INTERNET WITHOUT FEAR!

Practical Tips and Activities for the Elementary Classroom

by Dr. Elizabeth Rhodes Offutt
and Charles R. Offutt

Good Apple

Editor: Alexandra Behr

Good Apple
23740 Hawthorne Blvd.
Torrance, CA 90505

ISBN 1–56417–853–6

3 4 5 6 7 8 9   MAL   01 00 99 98 97

CONTENTS

Introduction

Why Is Everyone Talking About the Internet?

The Internet provides an unlimited source of information and methods for teaching and sharing knowledge. Many educators are using the Internet to enrich their curriculum. However, some teachers may not be aware of what the Internet can provide. Let's start with three examples.

In Blacksburg, Virginia, second graders have worked on several technology-based projects. After reading "The Three Little Pigs," for example, children constructed and tested three consecutively stronger houses and shared their results electronically with other classes.

At Cedar Creek Elementary School in Austin, Texas, third graders study the history and culture of their local community in a project titled "Walk Back Through Time Through Technology." With TENET, the Texas educational on-line service, they request historical facts about other communities and receive answers via electronic mail (e-mail).

The Boone School in Kansas City, Missouri, is near the start of the Oregon Trail, used by settlers in the late 1800s. Fourth-grade students at Boone are conducting research on the Internet and sending e-mail to other schools located on or near the Oregon Trail. They are inviting students at other schools to explore the West as part of an "on-line wagon train."

The preceding examples, two of which are highlighted in Odvard Egil Dyrli's "Teacher-Initiated Telecommunications Projects," *Technology & Learning,* April 1995, demonstrate how teachers and students can integrate e-mail and the Internet into their classroom activities.

Joining the Global Classroom

The Internet enables people to exchange ideas and information quickly throughout the world. Through cross-cultural exposure, students learn about people who may have different cultures and beliefs but who also share common experiences, feelings, and goals.

In "Four Days That Changed the World," Paul J. McCarty describes how the Internet made current events tangible to sixth graders in Salt Lake City. The students had been using e-mail to communicate with Russian students. During the 1991 counterrevolution in the former Soviet Union, the e-mail stopped. The Salt Lake City students were thrilled when they finally received a message. To help their Russian friends who were cut off from news, they sent news reports and words of encouragement. McCarty states: ". . . the former 6th graders who participated in (the events) believe to this day that they helped change the course of Russia's history."

NetNotes

Navigating the Internet should not be perceived as impossibly difficult and abstract for the average person. Your Internet skills will improve each time you work through the directories and searches. You'll find that students will enjoy using their detective skills to discover topics that interest them.

Benefits for Students

Sometimes adults underestimate young students' abilities to learn the basics of computers and the Internet. Most children can learn new languages quickly. The Internet is simply another language—one that can serve them in many areas of their lives for years to come.

The Internet provides students with audio, visual, and kinesthetic experiences. Students may develop sophisticated search-and-retrieval strategies as they explore new topics. The Internet can help strengthen students' critical-thinking skills. Finding appropriate resources on the Internet can test students' problem-solving abilities. They may also make judgments as to the value of the data they receive.

Making contacts around the world through e-mail can make most projects more interesting. Students are encouraged to work cooperatively while seeking and sharing information beyond their classroom. They can exchange several letters with Internet pen pals in the same amount of time that it would take for a regularly mailed letter to make a one-way trip.

Benefits for Teachers

The Internet brings to teachers and their students resources, tools, world-wide contacts, and challenging projects. The constraints of time and space are not as relevant on the Internet. France is just as close as the building next door. E-mail arrives in minutes, and vast files of valuable information can be copied in seconds.

The Internet can provide teachers with access to old friends and help them make new contacts. Teacher isolation becomes a thing of the past. Ideas are updated often and new information is distributed to Internet users very quickly. Sending mail to hundreds of people is no more time-consuming than sending a single message.

Through e-mail, parents and teachers can communicate directly. Teachers can send messages and assignments to children who have a modem at home. Students can e-mail letters or stories to their parents from school and get responses in person or through a return e-mail message.

Benefits for Parents and Guardians

Families have much to gain through use of the Internet. If there is a computer and Internet connection at home, family members can explore the Internet and learn with their children. They can join other educational communities throughout the world. Students can see school and home as one connected and cooperative learning environment.

Parents may have conflicting emotions about the Internet. Sometimes there is more negative publicity surrounding the Internet than positive. Parents—and all responsible adults—may be concerned about what is "out there" in cyberspace. Although some areas of the Internet are not meant for children, there is also an endless supply of resources that will benefit any child. Children should be encouraged and taught how to reach the valuable educational tools on the Internet. It should function as an extension of the classroom. Just as children are not left unsupervised in the classroom, they should not be left alone while wandering through cyberspace.

NetNotes

Parents or guardians may wish to establish the same guidelines for the Internet as they do for television or videos. There are software and other resources that block certain material from being viewed by children. Usually in those areas, a password would be required.

Benefits for Administrators

Administrators can use the Internet to offset budgetary considerations. Educators can utilize the many free educational resources on the Internet in their teaching and preparation of teaching materials. For instance, teachers may find free computer software that would help students learn a concept or skill.

The Internet can also help implement staff development. Discussion lists, electronic journals, and newsletters can broaden a teacher's knowledge of current issues in education. Administrators can use the Internet to follow the most current and effective research on teaching and learning strategies. Participation in discussion lists fosters exchanges of research ideas with peers from other universities and colleges.

The Internet gives all students an equal chance to access information. For those schools with limited funding, there are many telecommunication grants to facilitate purchases. Also, schools that teach at-risk students can obtain funding through various agencies. The *Grantwriter's Newsletter of Funding Resources* is a monthly publication that lists grants, contests, and corporate, foundation, and federal funding opportunities for K–12 schools. For information, write Education Retrieval Resource, 617 Wright Avenue, Terrytown, LA 70056–4037, or call 1–800–891–6354.

Another place to investigate potential funding sources is the U.S. Department of Education, Office of Educational Technology, 600 Independence Ave. SW, Room 6236, Washington, DC 20202.

Once your students have access to the Internet, they will not just have one library to turn to for information. They can turn to thousands of libraries, museums, resources, databases, and experts in every field.

Using This Book

Internet Without Fear! helps elementary teachers understand how to use the Internet, discusses the educational values of the Internet, and provides dozens of activities that can be incorporated throughout the curriculum.

Teachers must determine how to deal with the masses of retrieved information from the Internet, just as they would if their classroom were suddenly filled with thousands of books, videos, encyclopedias, magazines, and tickets to museums. Keep the following hints in mind.

- Read, skim, or try out everything you find.

- Internet addresses are subject to change. Seek out new sources to keep information up-to-date.

- If possible, develop a "buddy" system with other teachers so everyone can benefit from what each other finds.

- After some trial and error, you will soon find the best sites to use in your classroom. Teachers of younger students will need to do the initial browsing and exploring. Older students, with supervision, can find Internet locations easily.

- Be aware of how students respond to the resources they find. Some Internet sites will be instant hits, and some will not appeal at all.

- You can keep a log to record the effectiveness of the resources and display it in the classroom.

Part 1 contains a glossary and information to help you learn about and use the Internet. Part 2 contains many resources to help you integrate e-mail and other aspects of the Internet throughout your curriculum. After carefully reading Part 1, locate some of the resources in Part 2. In the process, you will discover more resources on your own. For instance, activities labeled "Treasure Chest Site" have links to hundreds more. Good luck during your voyages and adventures through cyberspace! And be sure to visit our Web site at *http://www.sselem.com* for Internet address updates.

Chapter 1
Internet Glossary

It is likely that the buzzwords associated with the Internet won't appear in your classroom dictionary. The following glossary introduces you to the most helpful terms. More detailed definitions appear throughout the next few chapters.

Archie: a program used to search for files at FTP sites. An Archie server has lists of files throughout the Internet. See also **FTP**.

baud rate: the numbers of bits of data that a modem can transmit per second.

bulletin board: a computer service dialed into by phone and modem. Bulletin boards allow users to post and retrieve messages.

cyberspace: data created by the millions of on-line computers. Coined by novelist William Gibson.

CPU: central processing unit. The core of a computer, it performs the computations directed by software commands.

dial-in: to connect to a computer by telephone and modem.

dial-up: to have your computer and modem dial a phone number and connect to another modem and computer.

download: to receive a file sent from another computer.

e-mail: electronic mail. To send or receive messages via computers on a network; the system of sending such messages.

FTP: file transfer protocol. A standardized, text-based method of transferring files between computers.

Gopher: a search-and-retrieval Internet tool with access to databases, text files, and other resources.

hardware: the physical pieces of equipment that comprise your computer system.

home page: often, the top document in a series of linked documents under a common Internet address; also called a Web page. Each home page has links to other home pages.

HTML: hypertext markup language. A set of ASCII characters that creates a hypertext document when embedded in a text document and interpreted by Web browser software. See also **hypertext**.

hyperlink: a way to connect different hypertext documents on the World Wide Web. Hyperlinks appear as highlighted text or graphics that are specially encoded.

hypermedia: Internet documents that consist primarily of hyperlinked sounds and images.

hypertext: files of text, sounds, images, and actions linked through specially encoded text or graphics. Users can browse related topics in any order.

information superhighway: as coined by Vice President Gore, a high-speed fiber-optic communications system that, when built, will form the core of the national information infrastructure.

Internet: a noncommercial, self-governing collection of computer networks devoted mostly to communication and research. It is not an on-line service and has no central computer.

Internet service provider: a commercial provider of Internet connections. Gives user a phone number to call, an account, and sometimes the software to establish an Internet connection and an e-mail mailbox.

LAN: local area network. Computers in a small geographic area, such as a school. LANs share data over private communication links.

MB: megabytes. One million bytes. The storage capacity of magnetic media such as floppy disks, hard disks, and memory.

modem: modulation/demodulation. A device that lets computers communicate over a telephone line.

network: computers and peripherals connected by permanent cables or by temporary connections made through telephone or other communication links.

post office: also called a mail server. A dedicated computer on the Internet with software to handle e-mail.

PPP: Point-to-Point Protocol. Allows dial-up access to the Internet. An alternative to SLIP.

RAM: random-access memory. The part of a computer's memory used for documents and programs. RAM is erased when the computer is turned off.

server: a computer dedicated to servicing requests from users at a high rate of demand. Servers often have massive storage capacities and high processing speeds.

SLIP: Serial Line Interface Protocol. Allows dial-up access to the Internet. An alternative to PPP.

software: the programs and applications that run on the computer.

surf: to browse the Internet using Web browser software.

system administrator: the person responsible for the computers and networks at businesses or schools.

telnet: Unix utility telephone network. The central part of Internet services, it lets users log in to another computer remotely.

UNIX: the Internet's operating system. The Unix operating system, developed in the late 1960s by Bell Laboratories, can run on multiple computer processors, even IBM compatibles and Apple Macintoshes.

upgrade: to acquire new versions of software and hardware.

upload: to transmit a file on your computer to another computer.

URL: Uniform Resource Locator. A naming, or addressing, protocol for computers connected to the Internet.

Veronica: a keyword-based program that searches Gopher servers for files. With Veronica, users are given lists of URL addresses and can then contact sites via FTP. See also **FTP**.

WAIS: Wide Area Information Servers. A search-and-retrieval Internet tool with more than 500 databases, it searches entire documents, not just titles. With WAIS, users can view documents (with Gopher, users just view the indexes of documents). See also **Gopher**.

WAN: wide area network. Covers a larger area than LAN; WANs share data over public communication links.

Web: another term for World Wide Web. See also **WWW**.

Web browser: software that surfs the Internet. When the user provides a URL, a Web browser connects to a remote computer and displays its home page.

WWW: World Wide Web. A network-wide, menu-based program providing hypertext and hypermedia links to other information sources throughout the Internet.

Chapter 2
What Is the Internet?

In the 1970s the United States Defense Department established links among huge research labs so that their computer networks could communicate. The project was expanded to take advantage of computerized radio and satellite links. In the 1980s the National Science Foundation established a high-speed network after the early sites converted to the Internet. Then new companies began to sell gateway technology so many more computer networks could have easy access to the Internet.

The Internet represents a worldwide collection of computer networks connected by special phone lines, satellites, microwave relays, fiber optics, and sophisticated software. The Internet also represents the millions of people who use it. Once on the Internet, users have access to the thousands of files put into the public domain. They can also send messages, talk online, get free software, and receive up-to-date news. The Internet has allowed a global community to form with the common vision of sharing knowledge and information.

The two most common networks are LANs and WANs. LANs, or local area networks, share data among personal computers and workstations over private communication links. WANs, or wide area networks, are groups of LANs linked with a common purpose. WANs share data over public communication links, such as long-distance telephone lines operated by commercial carriers. Each computer network is a small collection of computers connected electronically and able to communicate, making the Internet an *inter*connection of *net*works.

Each computer or network connected to the Internet (also called a *host*) is like a library. Its holdings might include text, graphics, and even video and audio recordings. Using the Internet is very much like traveling to libraries in your community, except you don't need a vehicle—just a computer and modem. The term *information superhighway* aptly describes the route on which you explore the Internet.

If you drew a dot for each library on the Internet and connected the dots with lines, you would create a giant spider web. In fact, one of the most popular ways to explore the Internet is through the World Wide Web.

World Wide Web

The World Wide Web, also known as WWW or the Web, is a collection of hypertext-linked Internet documents. Hypertext is a way to connect related pieces of information in computer databases or documents so users can peruse and retrieve information in random order. In the hypertext are hyperlinks—specially notated text or graphics. The special notation is written in HTML—hypertext markup language. Clicking a hyperlink takes you to a related document automatically, where you will find more hyperlinks. You can always return to the original document.

WWW allows you to make links between computers automatically, without knowing the addresses in advance. A hyperlink may also cause an audio recording or video clip to be played. These types of hyperlinks are called hypermedia. Hyperlinks make exploring the Internet easy. One minute you may be reading a document on medical schools through an Internet host at the University of Alabama; with a click of the mouse, you can view the medical school curriculum and faculty listing for the Sorbonne in Paris through an Internet host at the Sorbonne. More about how to access and surf the Internet may be found in the section entitled "Shopping List for Internet Access" (see page 24).

Uniform Resource Locators

Computers on the Internet that want to act like libraries are called hosts, and every host computer has a unique address. You can connect to a host by using its address, called a URL (Uniform Resource Locator). Part Two provides many URLs that lead to resources specific to curriculum areas. There are also many books available that serve as Internet Yellow Pages.

If the Internet's a Library, Where's the Card Catalog?

If you have ever visited a large library for the first time, you might have wondered how to get around and how to find what you want. The Internet can produce a similar feeling. Fortunately the Internet has numerous tools to help you find what you need.

Gopher: Gopher is a way to browse lots of information on the Internet. Organizations and individuals throughout the world have set up Gopher servers with menus of items. (A server is a computer with special software installed.) Double-clicking on a menu retrieves the item. Sometimes the item is text; sometimes it is another set of menus. One strength of Gopher is its ability for a menu to point to a different Gopher server—one in the next room or even in the next country. (Why "Gopher"? The Golden Gopher is the mascot of the University of Minnesota, where the Gopher system was developed.)

Most of the searches in a Gopher area use WAIS databases (Wide Area Information Servers). WAIS, originally designed for massively parallel supercomputers, is a very efficient way to search through huge amounts of information. WAIS databases are now found throughout the Internet. Many times the icons you see in Gopher point to a WAIS database or a list of WAIS databases.

Gopher and WAIS complement one another as you search the Internet. Gopher is like a book's table of contents, while WAIS is the index. Although your topic may not be discussed with enough depth to make it into the table of contents, you can still look in the index and perhaps find references to your topic.

Veronica: As a Gopher server is like a book's table of contents, Veronica is a way to find books on a particular topic so that their tables of contents can be searched. Veronica provides the means to locate Gopher servers on a particular topic. You can search by a general topic, or if you know the name of a Gopher server or menu, Veronica will help you locate it.

FTP: FTP (file transfer protocol) is one of the basic tools used on the Internet. Protocol describes how two computers talk to each other. Using FTP you can download, or copy to your computer, files from remote computers and upload, or copy from your computer, files to computers to which you have access. Files can consist of software, text, and graphics.

Early Internet users developed FTP so that researchers could copy files from one place to another. If there is software you want, you can copy it from an FTP site—a computer on the Internet dedicated as a file server.

FTP sites usually have names or addresses separated by periods, or "dots." For example, **ftp.aol.com** is the America Online FTP site. It is pronounced "F-T-P dot A-O-L dot Com."

Remember Veronica? Well, as you might guess, wherever Veronica is, you are sure to find Archie.

Archie: Archie is a way to search for and locate FTP sites. Much as Veronica searches for Gopher servers, Archie searches for FTP sites. Most FTP sites will have a help file, README file, or an INDEX file that provides information about the site. These text files can be viewed while still connected to the FTP site. Note, however, that just text files can be viewed this way, not the actual files you might want to download.

Telnet: Telnet allows users to log onto another computer on the network. With telnet, users can read files and data and use the remote computer's other services, sometimes even running software packages. Access is usually granted on a guest basis, meaning you have limited capabilities. You will need the computer's Internet address, the guest log-in name, and the password. Often the log-in name is *guest* and will not require a password. The site will provide access instructions.

You may be asked to register the first time you connect to a remote computer through telnet. Having guests register is how remote sites monitor the use of their resources. If you register, you may be able to create a personal log-in name and password for future use. Part Two will take you to several telnet sites for some fun activities and files to download.

Communicating on the Internet With E-Mail

Communicating with other Internet users through e-mail, or electronic mail, is one of the fastest-growing areas of the Internet. The section entitled "Making Your First Connection to Cyberspace" (see page 34) discusses the details of e-mail and provides some entertaining activities for you and your students.

Chapter 3
Shopping List for Internet Access

If you already have computer resources in your classroom or at your school, you might be tempted to skip this chapter. However, read on and you may gain a better understanding of your computer equipment.

The shopping list for Internet-related hardware and software isn't long. However, you will encounter trade-offs between money spent and advantages gained. The following list presents the basic requirements. Some items can be satisfied in multiple ways, so a few examples of each will be given. A helpful source for more information would be the systems administrator for your school or district. A systems administrator purchases, sets up, controls, and installs software on computers.

Internet Access

There are four primary ways to connect with the Internet.

Shell Account: A shell account is an entry-level Internet access account. It is good for accessing text, not graphics. With a shell account, you dial into a host computer operated by an Internet service provider instead of connecting your computer directly to the Internet. Access costs are based on the amount of usage.

SLIP/PPP: Serial Line Interface Protocol/Point-to-Point Protocol is a step up from the shell account. With a SLIP/PPP connection, your computer system connects directly to the Internet. Your computer talks on the Internet in the same language as other computers on the Internet. This provides a faster throughput of data. You may still use an Internet service provider, but your dial-in connection is made to a SLIP/PPP connection rather than accessing the Internet from within a shell.

SLIP/PPP connections are typically much faster and more reliable than the standard modem connection. The costs of a SLIP/PPP connection are higher than a shell account. Certain commercial on-line services, such as CompuServe, allow a dial-in PPP connection if you have the appropriate software on your PC. Your service provider will tell you which connection you need.

Commercial On-line Gateway Service: If you subscribe to a commercial on-line gateway service, such as America Online or CompuServe, you connect to the Internet by locating the Internet service feature while on-line. See the section entitled "Commercial On-line Services" (page 48) for information about on-line services.

Leased Phone Line: A leased phone line provides more speed and power than other connections. Large companies or universities often use leased lines, since they have many users in multiple sites and have lots of data to send. A leased line resembles a SLIP/PPP connection because the LAN is connected directly to the Internet. However, the cost is much higher. Some leased lines may cost as much as $10,000 per year.

Computer

The computer unit is the central item of your Internet connection. Your computer will most likely be a personal computer. Throughout this book, we will refer to personal computers as PCs, with no inference to a particular brand. Separate references will indicate specific versions of software or certain hardware components. Remember, the Internet will never care what kind of computer you are using. One of the original goals of the Internet was to create a common denominator in software to make communication not dependent on the computer used.

A few important characteristics of your computer are listed below.

Processor Speed: The faster the better is a good approach with computer processor speeds. However, faster also means costlier. Processor speeds are advertised in MHz (megahertz). Typical speeds range from 25 MHz for older Macintosh systems to 200 MHz for the new Intel Pentium Pro and Motorola PowerPC chips. These speeds will continue to increase.

If you connect to the Internet through a telephone dial-up line, you are restricted somewhat by your modem's speed. No matter how fast your computer's processor speed is, information can come to you only as fast as the modem can deliver it. Besides, the applications that require fast processor speeds are not necessarily the ones used during an Internet session. However, as more people surf the Internet and sophisticated commercial uses increase, the need for offload processing, or letting your computer do the work of downloading instead of the host computer, has become necessary.

When selecting a computer for Internet use, purchase one that has multimedia applications. This will help you display graphics on your monitor as quickly as they are downloaded to your computer. To this end, the more important characteristic of your computer is how much memory it has.

RAM: Random access memory is the part of your computer used for documents and programs. The more memory you have in your computer, the more things it can do at one time. Most Internet communication software packages will recommend a minimum RAM requirement, which you should try to exceed. Consider a minimum of 12 MB to 16 MB.

RAM is measured in megabytes, or 1 million bytes. Therefore, 16 MB of RAM represents 16 million bytes of memory. Computer information in RAM is stored as a combination of ones and zeros. Each one or zero represents a bit, and there are eight bits in a byte. Each byte can be thought of as a single character in a text string. Sixteen million times 8 bits is a lot of information!

Hard Drive: A hard drive, or hard disk, is a way for your computer to store information. A hard drive or disk is measured by how many bytes of information it can store, usually in megabytes. Typical hard drives range from 540 MB to 1 gigabyte (1 billion bytes) or larger.

One of the great uses of the Internet is downloading information onto your computer to use later. Therefore, the larger the hard disk, the more information you can store. Be careful, though. A large hard disk is a lot like a large storage closet. Once you begin to fill it, it may never get cleaned out.

Talk to your system administrator about how to back up your hard disk. You might copy the information to a secondary location, such as a DAT, for safekeeping. DATs (digital audio tapes) can hold several gigabytes of information.

Monitor: A high-resolution color monitor will greatly enhance your enjoyment of the Internet. A 15-inch monitor is standard and sufficient for most PCs. You may wish to have a 21-inch high-resolution monitor if your students need to gather around just one computer. However, the cost of a 21-inch monitor can exceed the cost of the computer. You might consider buying a less expensive device that displays the video output of your computer from an overhead transparency machine.

Keyboard: Any standard or extended computer keyboard is acceptable.

Mouse/Trackball/Trackpad: A mouse is almost a necessity with today's point-and-click software design. Another pointing device is the trackball/trackpad. If desk space is at a premium, you may wish to purchase one or the other.

Speakers: A set of good external speakers on your PC is recommended because of the audio resources on the Internet. Some newer multimedia computers may have the speakers provided. For non-Macintosh computers without built-in speakers, you may need to purchase a sound card, which installs in the back of the computer, to provide a connection for external speakers.

29

Modem

To connect to the Internet through a dial-up service, you need a modem. It converts your computer's signals into signals that can be sent over the telephone line. Another modem on the other end converts the telephone line signal into a computer signal. A modem allows you to download or upload files.

Modems differ in their speeds, or how fast they can transfer data. The unit of measurement for modem speed is baud rate. Though not technically correct, baud rate generally refers to the bits per second (bps) that can be transmitted or received by the modem.

A modem rated at 14,400 bps, or 14.4 Kbps, can transmit 14,400 bits of information—about 1,800 characters per second. A full page of English text is roughly 2,000 characters, so a 14,400 bps modem can transmit about 60 pages of text in a minute. If you used a 2,400 bps modem, 60 pages of text would take nearly 24 minutes to transmit.

Since most Internet service providers charge $10 to $15 per hour connected, buying a high-speed modem is wise. If you have to connect to a long-distance phone line, slow modems can be very costly. The fastest modems for standard telephone lines are 28,800 bps modems; they are the recommended choice for Internet services. These modems can also compress data and do error correction, so the actual data throughput may be higher. The cost difference between a 2,400 bps and a 28,800 bps modem is several hundred dollars.

Network Adapter

A network adapter is a circuit board installed inside your computer. It allows you to be hard-wired to a local area network within your school. Your LAN may be connected to the Internet already, or you may wish to discuss getting a hard-wired connection for your school with your system administrator.

The fastest way to be connected to the Internet is to be hard-wired. Hardwiring implies your computer is connected directly to the Internet. It isn't. Hardwired connections require a high-speed phone line that allows for multiple computers to access the Internet at the same time. The telephone connection is through a special computer on your school's network, not through a modem on your classroom's computer.

Printer

Do not underestimate the importance of a fast, high-resolution printer. Many documents you may wish to print from the Internet contain graphics. These graphics will not reproduce well from a dot-matrix printer. A color ink-jet printer or a gray-scale laser printer is ideal. Once again, speed is important. Printers are usually rated in pages per minute. A four-page-per-minute printer is typical. Some color ink-jet printers may print at three minutes per page, but the color output is often worth the wait. Many high-resolution printers can print on overhead transparency films.

Communication Software

The software required to get your computer connected to the Internet will depend on your computer and your method of gaining access to the Internet. If you have an IBM-compatible PC, you must have at least Windows 3.1 installed. With a Macintosh, the operating system software is already set up to run Internet software. Your school's system administrator or your Internet service provider can describe the required software. Depending on your service provider, your subscription will likely include all the required software you need.

Many service providers are listed and advertise on the Internet. You can also look for names in computer magazines, such as *Internet Magazine, PC Week, PC World, MacWeek, BYTE,* or *PC Computing.*

Web Browser

Web browser software is a necessity for surfing the Internet. It provides a user-friendly interface to the World Wide Web. Web browsers such as NCSA Mosaic™ or Netscape Navigator™ are two of the more popular packages. See the section on browsing the Web at the end of Chapter 4 (page 42).

A Web browser is probably the best way to learn just how much the Internet has to offer. It lets you explore the Internet through URLs and hypertext links. You can use one of the many keyword search utilities, such as Lycos™, to search for Web pages.

NetNotes

Most Internet access software packages are free to educational institutions. Local universities can provide information and help and may even let you establish a dial-in account through them to the Internet. However, these accounts are getting more difficult to obtain since so many people are joining the Internet.

Chapter 4
Making Your First Connection to Cyberspace

This chapter assumes that you have obtained all the hardware and software necessary to access the Internet. You will first learn about e-mail, an easy and fun way to use the Internet. Then we will discuss using the Web browser Netscape Navigator to explore the World Wide Web.

E-Mail: The Cyberspace Postal Service

Many business and universities use e-mail internally to communicate memos and letters. A paper copy of an e-mail message can always be printed. E-mail software exists for many types of computer systems; most operate on the same principles. If you have

NetNotes

The following e-mail discussion applies whether you have access to e-mail from an Internet service provider, a commercial on-line service, or a commercial provider of e-mail services. Just the software needed to access e-mail will change.

computers at your school, check with the system administrator about your e-mail capabilities. If your school is connected to the Internet already, the system administrator can set up your class for e-mail.

Your Internet service provider or school system administrator should provide you with an e-mail address or addresses and the appropriate software to access e-mail. If your classroom has a direct connection to the Internet, you will not need a modem. However, if your Internet service is through dial-up access, your e-mail software will use a modem and telephone line. If you do not have Internet access yet, you can still send e-mail with a commercial on-line service such as America Online or CompuServe.

How to Address E-mail

Each person is assigned an e-mail account and an e-mail address. If you already have e-mail at your school, don't confuse that e-mail address with an Internet or on-line service e-mail address. Your address might be your first and middle initial and last name. It will also include the address of your service provider. Your service provider will act like a post office and postal carrier, collecting and distributing mail as it is received to anyone who has an account.

The standard format for e-mail addresses is shown below.
Note the two major parts: who and where.

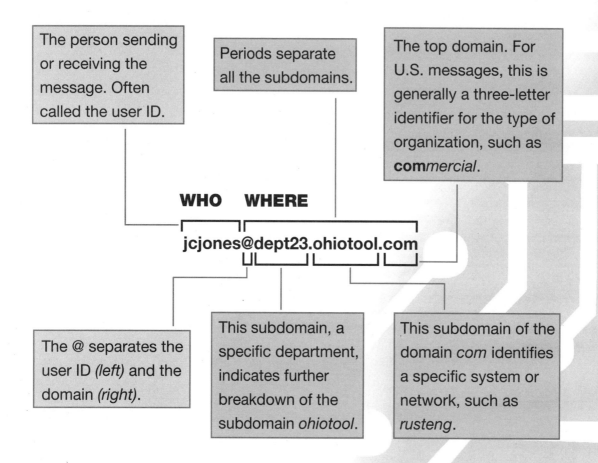

Systems on the Internet read addresses from right to left, with
information becoming more specific toward the left. At the far
right of an Internet address is the country where the e-mail
originated, usually a two-letter designation. If there is no country
code, the message comes from within the United States.

To the left of the country code, if there is one, are two or three
letters that signify the type of organization the e-mail originated

from. In the preceding example, *.com* means the e-mail is from a commercial or business account. Other organization codes are *.edu*, an educational site; *.gov*, a U.S. government site; *.mil*, a U.S. military site; *.net*, a network site; and *.org*, a private or nonprofit organization.

Internet users and users of various on-line services can send each other e-mail. An America Online user with an e-mail address of jrbrown@aol.com can send e-mail to a CompuServe user at the address 12345.6789@compuserve.com. On-line services use the Internet to deliver their e-mail messages to other on-line service providers. The Internet uses the Domain Name System to address e-mail. This is the same format used to send e-mail between on-line services.

Many Internet addresses, such as *dept23.ohiotool.com*, include words or abbreviations so that people can remember them more easily. Computers actually have numeric Internet addresses. The form of these numeric addresses is standard and has the following format, 123.456.789.001, which is pronounced "one two three dot four five six dot seven eight nine dot zero zero one." The Domain Name Server looks up the alphabetic form of the address and converts it to the numeric form. You may run across a numeric address of an Internet site. You can use either form.

How to Send Your First Message

To send e-mail, you need the address of the person or persons you wish to communicate with. In the appropriate fields, enter the address of the recipient (TO:), the address of anyone you wish to receive a courtesy copy (cc:), the subject, and the text of your message.

The FROM: field, not usually seen, will be created automatically based on the account used to send the e-mail. Most e-mail software allows you to create custom address books for storing e-mail addresses. You can usually reference these addresses by a real name, such as John Brown, and the address book will substitute John Brown's e-mail address.

You may have multiple e-mail addresses, in which case you would create multiple entries in the address book. For example, (Your name)—work, (Your name)—school, (Your name)—AOL. Many e-mail software packages allow you to create groups, or mailing lists, in the address book. A group is a subset of previously entered individual addresses saved under a single name. For example, *Second Grade* may point to seven e-mail addresses. By placing the group name in the TO: field, you don't have to enter the seven addresses separately. The same feature can be used in the cc: field.

The area set aside for the text of your message works like a simple word processor. Once you have entered the desired text, send the e-mail with the appropriate command or keystroke. Most software will not keep a copy of your message. If you wish to retain a copy of e-mail you send, you can save the message in a draft folder or cc: yourself.

Retrieving E-mail

Almost all e-mail packages will have an inbox, an outbox, and a trash can. E-mail sent to you on a LAN either will be waiting for you in an inbox or you may have to request new messages to be loaded. Commercial on-line services will inform you that you have mail waiting when you sign on. Some services, such as America Online and CompuServe, use a voice message.

You will usually see a list of received mail. The list will indicate who the mail is from, the subject, and maybe the date it was sent. After you read your mail, you can save it or trash it. If your software can create folders, you may wish to organize your incoming mail messages by subject. Keeping messages requires storage space on your computer or the computer used for your mail service. Some services require that mail not be kept longer than a certain time. E-mail is like other tools used in your teaching—the more organized you keep it, the more useful it is.

E-mail Activities

Activity: Global Grocery List (GGL)

Location: dwarlick%ncsdpi.fred.org@cerf.net

Ask students to collect some local grocery prices for one week. For example: oranges, 3 for $1.00; cheese, $2.57 a pound; milk, $1.29 a half-gallon. Have students combine their lists and e-mail them to GGL. They can check their e-mail periodically to compare and contrast the price lists of other participants.

Activity: A World of Studies

Location: http://mypc.shastalink.k12.ca.us/www/ projectcity/pchome.html

Fourth-grade students at Project City Elementary School in Shasta Lake, California, are hosts to the World Wide Creative Writing Project. Students in Mr. Keeler's classroom have sent out story starters to classrooms around the world. After your students e-mail the hosts and choose a category, they can join the project.

NetNotes

If you have experience on the Internet, this section will be easy. If you are still confused about how to access e-mail or the Internet, read the preceding chapters before attempting these activities.

Your students will receive a story starter and will be asked to add the next paragraph. They should e-mail the new paragraph back to Mr. Keeler's classroom at the address on the Web page. The hosts will redirect the stories to other classrooms around the world. This e-mail process continues until there is a completed project. Your students will receive a copy of the finished story with a description of where their story traveled.

Activity: Emoticons
Location: Any e-mail address

As students become more comfortable with sending and receiving e-mail, they can add emoticons. An emoticon is a set of symbols created with regular computer keys. You will need to turn your head sideways to interpret them. For example, :-) is a smile and :-(is a frown. Provide the following examples, and encourage students to invent their own.

@—>— (a rose)
{{{{{{{{{{{{{{()}}}}}}}}}}}}}} (lots of hugs)
:-D (a large grin)
:-l ("I am not amused.")
:-) (a smile)

Browsing the Web

If you have access to the Internet, chances are you also have access to a Web browser software package. Two of the more popular ones are Netscape Navigator and NCSA Mosaic. Also, most of the more popular on-line services have their own Web browser software included. You may have to download some of the software to your computer the first time you use it, but simple instructions should be provided.

Each Web browser looks similar from the surface but will have special features and functions that will take you beyond the scope of our attention here. Advanced uses and understanding of Web browser software can be obtained from a user's manual or supplementary user's guides.

Let's assume you have Netscape Navigator installed on your PC. After running the Netscape application and connecting to the Internet, you will see the main window. The top region consists of several buttons.

back: goes back in the list of previously viewed URLs.

forward: goes forward in the list of previously viewed URLs.

home: goes to a Web page predefined by you. The default home URL is Netscape's Internet home page (www.netscape.com).

reload: reloads the currently listed URL address.

images: if the automatic loading of images is off, clicking this button causes images to download.

open: presents a dialog box that asks for a location, or URL address, to open.

print: prints the currently displayed Web page to your default printer.

find: searches for a word in the displayed document.

stop: cancels the data transfer in progress.

You will also see the Netscape logo, which will show stars falling across the sky when data is being received from the Internet. Other Web browser software packages use their logos here in similar ways.

Beneath the top row of buttons is a data entry field labeled *go to* or *location*. If you place your cursor in the field and delete current text, you can type in the URL address you wish to go to. If you have connected to a Web page via a hypertext link, this field will indicate the URL address of the document you are viewing. Remember, each address you go to is pointing to a specific HTML document you can view using the Web browser software.

Beneath the URL entry field are several more buttons to take you to specific areas on the Internet.

What's New: lists new URL addresses and Web sites. Continuously updated.

What's Cool: lists what Netscape believes to be unusual, intriguing sites. Updated routinely.

Handbook: has an index that should be skimmed before you look for information or help.

Net Search: allows you to search the Internet with keywords or even a question. You will receive a list of Web sites whose abstract descriptions contain the keywords you provided. Be careful; this search can turn up thousand of entries. Be as specific as possible.

Net Directory: a basic Yellow Pages to the Internet. Introduces you to Yahoo, currently the most popular Web site for finding what's on the Internet.

Newsgroups: connects you to your defined set of newsgroups. If you don't have any defined, you can subscribe to some during your first visit. Subscribing to newsgroups is a great way to obtain information.

The most important region of the Web browser window is the Web page viewing area. As each document loads to your computer, you can scroll down the page with the right-hand scroll bar. Since text is often loaded before images, you can skim the document to see if there is anything interesting. If not, you can click *STOP* to cancel the request. Once you click *STOP*, you can type in another URL address or return to the previous page by clicking *BACK*.

The Netscape menus are at the top of the screen. They are similar to most Windows or Macintosh menus. Many menu commands are identical to the buttons we have just discussed. One of the most important menu items is Bookmarks.

Bookmarks allow you to save URL addresses you have visited so you can revisit them without re-entering the address. If you pull down the Bookmarks menu, you can add a Bookmark or view your list of bookmarks. This list is stored on your PC and will be accessible each time you run your Web browser. If you want to visit a site each day, this handy tool can save time. Some browsers allow you to define sets of bookmarks so you, for instance, can have one list and students can have another. See the user's guide or pull down under *HELP* and search *bookmarks* for more information.

As you view each Web page, you will notice highlighted and/or underlined text and images. These represent the hyperlinks of the Web page. Clicking on any highlighted area will immediately connect you to the Web page identified by the link. If you visit a link and want to get back, simply click on the *BACK* button.

Your PC will most likely store the pages you visit, so as you go back and forth through your pages, they will load much more quickly the second time around. This technique is referred to as cache. It uses the PC memory and hard disk to temporarily store Web page information. If you quit the browser application and restart, you will lose the information in the cache memory.

The best way to learn about surfing the Internet and the World Wide Web is to simply do it. Don't be afraid to try new things and explore new paths. If you think you've gotten lost, you can always click on *HOME*.

Chapter 5
Commercial On-line Services

One way to obtain access to the Internet is through commercial on-line services. Three of the leading services and the highlights offered by them are described here. Others include eWorld from Apple Computer, Microsoft Network (MSN), and Genie. Part Two of *Internet Without Fear!* contains activities based on accessing certain areas of an on-line service.

America Online

America Online (AOL) is the fastest growing commercial on-line service. Since 1989, AOL has reportedly signed on nearly 3 million members. AOL is an icon-based, point-and-click interface that is very easy for non-computer experts to use.

AOL's Internet access, including a built-in World Wide Web browser, is one reason AOL is so popular. The Web browser and FTP capabilities add a worldwide network of downloadable files to AOL.

Without the Internet, AOL offers more than 50,000 shareware files and programs to download. Shareware is software normally obtained free for trial usage. If you decide to keep it, you must pay the author a small fee for licensing. This fee will usually pay for a manual, technical support, and notification of future updates.

Teachers will love the bulletin board feature of AOL, which allows the user to post messages on an electronic bulletin board. Other AOL visitors can then respond. It's like being able to send e-mail to everyone who might be interested in a certain topic without knowing his or her address.

AOL departments include the following:

FlashSession: allows the user to compose and to retrieve mail off-line (not dialed in). This feature will save considerable connect-time charges.

Today's News & Newsstand: provides on-line versions of many popular magazines, including *Time, Nickelodeon Magazine, Scientific America,* and *DC Comics Online*.

Personal Finance: gives user the ability to create a fictitious stock portfolio, track stock information, gather current financial news, and locate company profiles.

Clubs & Interests: allows people with common interests to take part in discussions electronically.

Computing: download software, contact many of the leading software and computer companies, send e-mail for technical assistance, and find out the latest computing news.

Travel: view pictures of travel destinations, read travel magazines, check the weather, and even check airline schedules.

Marketplace: includes electronic stores such as Kidsoft Superstore, OfficeMax Online, Tower Records, Online Bookstore, and Health & Vitamins Express.

People Connection: these chat rooms allow real-time conversations between a group of people, usually a maximum of 25. Chat rooms can get confusing when 25 different conversations appear on your screen at once!

Entertainment: offers information about movies, music, and theater. You can download movie clips, soundtrack samples, and other entertainment business advertising.

NetNotes

Movie clips and soundtracks can take a half-hour or more to download and can consume considerable hard disk space. You might consider downloading a movie release clip once a month. You do not need to be dialed into AOL to view the movie clip. You can download special software to view these items from AOL at just the on-line time cost.

Education & Reference Desk: offers on-line reference books, encyclopedias, *Smithsonian Online*, and much more. Part 2 of this book will take you into these two areas for some great classroom activities.

Internet Connection: allows access to the AOL Web browser. AOL has one of the better Web browsers of the commercial on-line services. The Internet area for AOL also includes a Newsgroup reader, FTP service, and Gopher access.

Newsgroups are similar to the message boards throughout America Online. Since these Newsgroups are distributed through the Internet, you'll find many more topics and millions of people in these globe-trotting discussions.

Sports: provides news, game scores, and discussion groups.

Kids Only: provides specialty magazines for kids, bulletin boards, and other features.

NetNotes

AOL, like all commercial on-line services, requires a password when dialing in. Protect this password, because on-line charges can accrue quickly. AOL even provides further security within the program to password-protect certain areas of the service. Look under the Members menu and select Parental Control after dialing into AOL.

CompuServe

CompuServe leans toward financial information, news, and reference material for businesses and professionals. Numerous forums provide information on computer hardware and software. Many software vendors provide free upgrades to their software through these forums.

The major subject areas of CompuServe include the following.

News, Weather & Sports: allows access to the latest information from Associated Press, United Press International, Reuters world wires, and more.

Magazines: users can read and retrieve articles from periodicals from around the world. There is an additional charge for this service.

Communicate: find e-mail, classified ads, special events and contests, and real-time discussions.

Computers: find forums, reference materials, technical support, articles, shareware, and products for more than 1,000 hardware and software companies.

Reference/Education: contains an extensive reference library of articles, directories, legal information, statistics, consumer information, and newsletters. Includes current and historical information. The on-line dictionary and encyclopedia are updated four times annually.

Professional & Finance: financial services that are tailored for the individual investor, providing stock quotes, brokerage services, business data, charts, and other analysis. Professionals can access information and exchange ideas through professional interest areas.

Internet: provides Internet access with Gopher access, FTP, and an integrated Web browser.

Travel: includes air, hotel, car, tour, and cruise information.

Shopping: offers access to more than 160 merchants, with no connect charges for browsing and ordering.

Home/Leisure: includes the areas of health and fitness, home and family, arts, hobbies, and outdoor activities.

Fun & Games: can provide hours of enjoyment. Includes software downloads such as demos and updates.

Entertainment: includes movie and music guides, featured artists, music vendor forums, and more.

Prodigy

Prodigy is sometimes called "an on-line service for novices." This is not meant to be critical. Prodigy is easy to install and provides numerous prompts and simple commands.

Prodigy contains several major areas.

News & Weather: provides on-line news and weather forecasts.

Business/Finance: provides the latest news on business and financial topics, stock quotes and charts, mutual funds, and corporate analysis.

Sports: gives you information on sports events and statistics. Includes color photos and graphics, pro scores, and stories while games are in play.

Communicate: provides real-time chat rooms, e-mail, bulletin boards, and access to Usenet newsgroups.

Entertainment: describes the latest movies, theater showings, and music releases.

MarketPlace: includes merchants, discount outlets, and specialty shops. Users can place classified ads on the MarketPlace bulletin board.

Computing: on-line information is available for all types of computers. Exchange ideas with other computer users, talk to experts to get advice and information, receive on-line technical support, read the latest releases of computer-oriented magazines, and connect to other computing-related Web sites.

Travel: allows you to make travel plans, check reservations, and view travel locations. City and vacation guides tell you what's hot and what's not according to other Prodigy members.

Internet: provides simple point-and-click access to Web pages. The Internet access requires just a single mouse click to take you to World Wide Web sites. A Personal Web Page feature allows you to create a site on the Internet.

Kids Zone & Teen Turf: contains child-oriented areas with games, on-screen activities, reference materials, Web sites, and bulletin boards. Parental access control is available.

PART 2 Integrating Internet Resources Throughout the Curriculum

In Part 2, Internet activities are integrated with reading; language arts; math; science; social studies; health, nutrition, and physical fitness; and music, art, and dance. The last chapter contains Gopher sites, Internet groups, mailing lists, and other resources of interest to educators. Internet sites and activities were chosen using these guidelines:

• The site contains several links to other valuable resources related to the subject area.

• The site provides a resource, software tool, or pool of knowledge difficult to obtain in other ways. Activities provide unique tools not found in traditional resources.

NetNotes

The Internet changes rapidly. Use the resources in this book but continue to explore the links found at most of the sites. Sometimes Internet sites are "down" for maintenance or too busy to accept your connection. Keep trying! If a site changes or is no longer available, don't give up. Use the Internet tools in this section to locate related areas.

• The site falls under several of the following philosophies: Students need developmentally appropriate activities for optimum growth. They need to be actively involved in learning. They need to construct their own knowledge. Classroom activities should excite children about learning.

Chapter 6
Reading

There are many Internet resources to help teach reading in the elementary classroom. The following are some of the most beneficial and enjoyable resources for K–6 teachers.

Reading Resources	K	1	2	3	4	5	6
Activities by the Letter	*	*					
Book Nook	*	*	*	*	*	*	*
Children's Literature	*	*	*	*	*	*	*
Children's Literature Home Page	*	*	*	*	*	*	*
Fonzo Explores the Universe	*	*	*	*	*	*	*
Helping Your Child Learn How to Read	*	*	*	*	*	*	*
Illustrated Children's Books	*	*	*	*			
An Indian in My Cupboard	*	*	*	*	*	*	*
Newbery Award Winning Books	*	*	*	*	*	*	*
Percussion Stories	*	*	*	*	*	*	*
Personalize Your Own Book	*	*	*	*			
Pigs	*	*	*	*			
Puns: Prose as Deadly Torture					*	*	*
Read Along Stories	*	*	*	*	*	*	*
The Realist Wonder Society	*	*	*	*	*	*	*
Shelves of Children's Literature	*	*	*	*	*	*	*
A Story as You Like It	*	*	*	*	*	*	*
Story Hour (The Internet Public Library)	*	*	*	*	*	*	*
Theodore Tugboat	*	*	*	*			
Young Authors Conference	*	*	*	*	*	*	*
	K	1	2	3	4	5	6

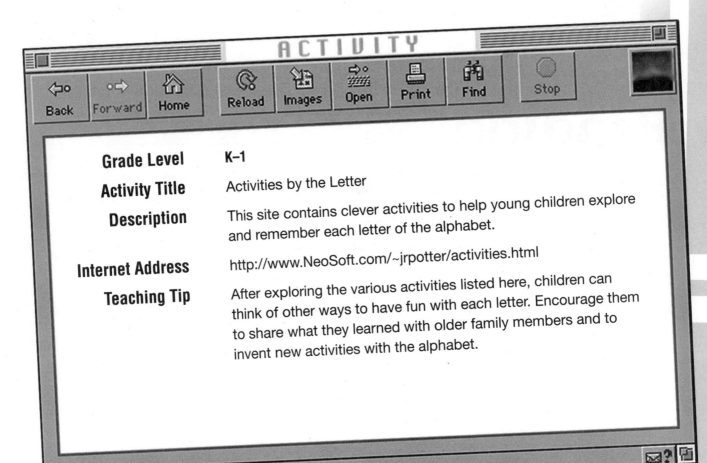

Grade Level   K–1

Activity Title   Activities by the Letter

Description   This site contains clever activities to help young children explore and remember each letter of the alphabet.

Internet Address   http://www.NeoSoft.com/~jrpotter/activities.html

Teaching Tip   After exploring the various activities listed here, children can think of other ways to have fun with each letter. Encourage them to share what they learned with older family members and to invent new activities with the alphabet.

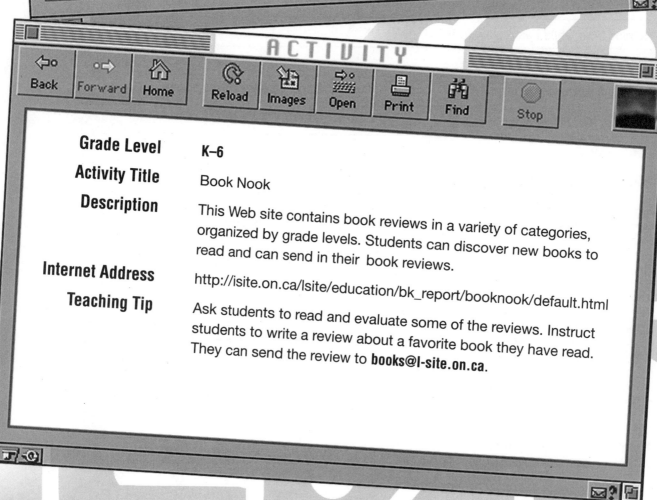

Grade Level   K–6

Activity Title   Book Nook

Description   This Web site contains book reviews in a variety of categories, organized by grade levels. Students can discover new books to read and can send in their book reviews.

Internet Address   http://isite.on.ca/lsite/education/bk_report/booknook/default.html

Teaching Tip   Ask students to read and evaluate some of the reviews. Instruct students to write a review about a favorite book they have read. They can send the review to **books@l-site.on.ca**.

Grade Level	K–6
Activity Title	Children's Literature
Description	This Web site lists numerous resources related to books for children and young adults. Students can click on "Tell Me More! About Children's Authors and Their Books" or go to the "Tell Me More" site. The latter site contains author biographies and information about fictional characters and settings.
Internet Address	http://www.ucalgary.ca/~dkbrown/index.html http://www.ucalgary.ca/~dkbrown/authors.html
Teaching Tip	"Tell Me More" site can be used with many books. If you are reading *Winnie-the-Pooh* with young students, help them find the title and click on the four categories. Children can find out how to play Virtual Pooh-Sticks, then teach the game to a partner.

Treasure Chest Site!

Grade Level	K–6
Activity Title	Children's Literature Home Page
Description	At this site more than 5,000 new children's books are reviewed each year. You will find reviews of electronic books and multimedia and profiles of prominent authors and illustrators.
Internet Address	http://www.parentsplace.com/readroom/childnew/index.html
Teaching Tip	This site can serve as a source of many forms of literature. If other resources in this chapter do not offer the book or literature you are seeking, try the address above.

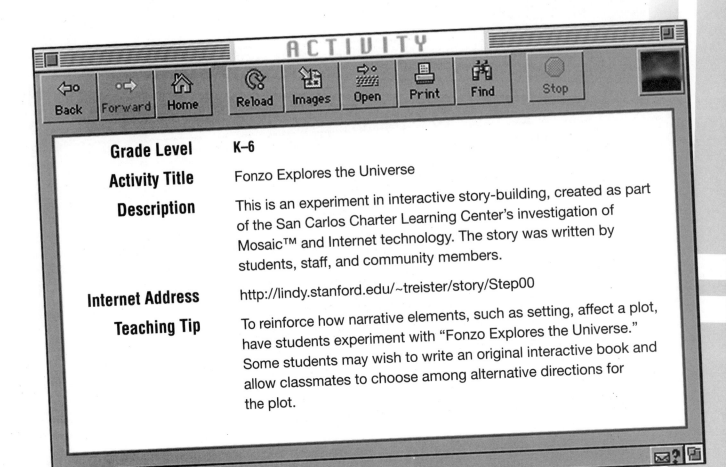

Grade Level   **K–6**

Activity Title   Fonzo Explores the Universe

Description   This is an experiment in interactive story-building, created as part of the San Carlos Charter Learning Center's investigation of Mosaic™ and Internet technology. The story was written by students, staff, and community members.

Internet Address   http://lindy.stanford.edu/~treister/story/Step00

Teaching Tip   To reinforce how narrative elements, such as setting, affect a plot, have students experiment with "Fonzo Explores the Universe." Some students may wish to write an original interactive book and allow classmates to choose among alternative directions for the plot.

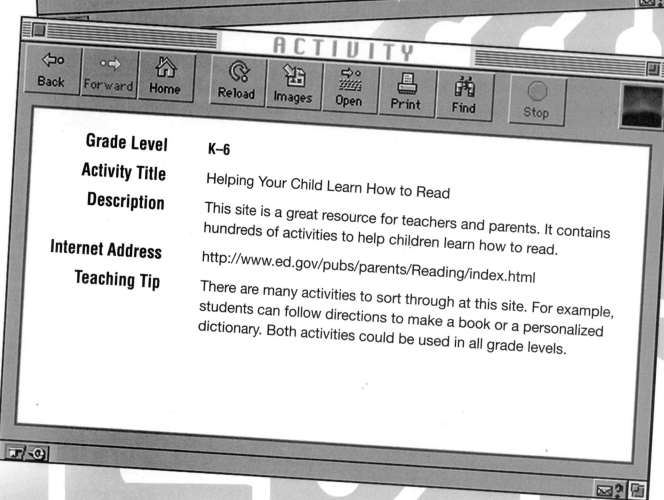

Grade Level   **K–6**

Activity Title   Helping Your Child Learn How to Read

Description   This site is a great resource for teachers and parents. It contains hundreds of activities to help children learn how to read.

Internet Address   http://www.ed.gov/pubs/parents/Reading/index.html

Teaching Tip   There are many activities to sort through at this site. For example, students can follow directions to make a book or a personalized dictionary. Both activities could be used in all grade levels.

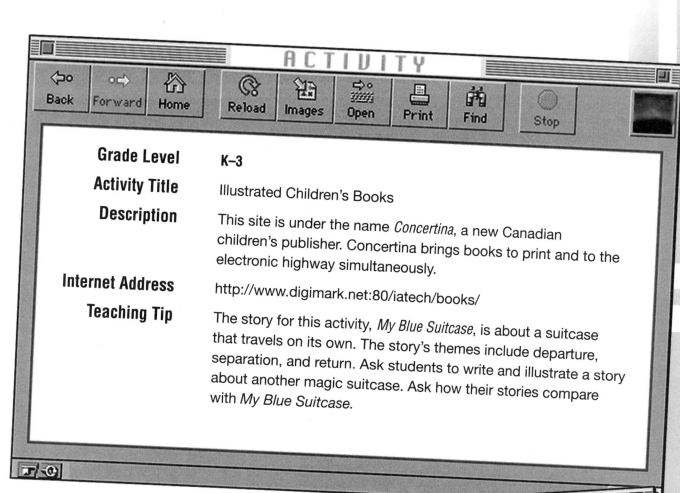

ACTIVITY

Grade Level	K–3
Activity Title	Illustrated Children's Books
Description	This site is under the name *Concertina*, a new Canadian children's publisher. Concertina brings books to print and to the electronic highway simultaneously.
Internet Address	http://www.digimark.net:80/iatech/books/
Teaching Tip	The story for this activity, *My Blue Suitcase*, is about a suitcase that travels on its own. The story's themes include departure, separation, and return. Ask students to write and illustrate a story about another magic suitcase. Ask how their stories compare with *My Blue Suitcase*.

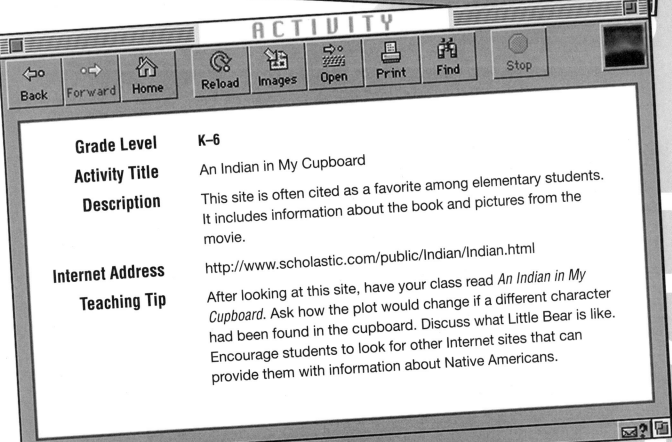

ACTIVITY

Grade Level	K–6
Activity Title	An Indian in My Cupboard
Description	This site is often cited as a favorite among elementary students. It includes information about the book and pictures from the movie.
Internet Address	http://www.scholastic.com/public/Indian/Indian.html
Teaching Tip	After looking at this site, have your class read *An Indian in My Cupboard*. Ask how the plot would change if a different character had been found in the cupboard. Discuss what Little Bear is like. Encourage students to look for other Internet sites that can provide them with information about Native Americans.

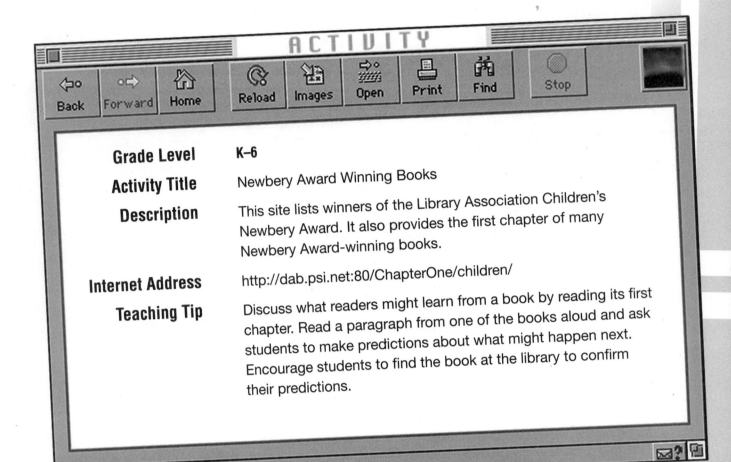

Grade Level   **K–6**

Activity Title   Newbery Award Winning Books

Description   This site lists winners of the Library Association Children's Newbery Award. It also provides the first chapter of many Newbery Award-winning books.

Internet Address   http://dab.psi.net:80/ChapterOne/children/

Teaching Tip   Discuss what readers might learn from a book by reading its first chapter. Read a paragraph from one of the books aloud and ask students to make predictions about what might happen next. Encourage students to find the book at the library to confirm their predictions.

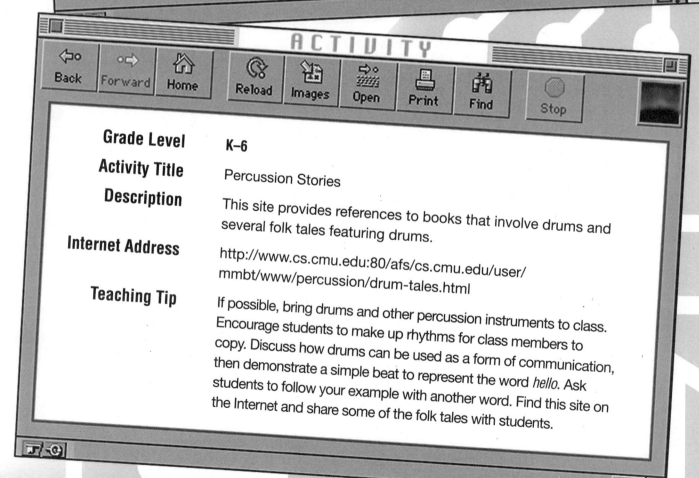

Grade Level   **K–6**

Activity Title   Percussion Stories

Description   This site provides references to books that involve drums and several folk tales featuring drums.

Internet Address   http://www.cs.cmu.edu:80/afs/cs.cmu.edu/user/mmbt/www/percussion/drum-tales.html

Teaching Tip   If possible, bring drums and other percussion instruments to class. Encourage students to make up rhythms for class members to copy. Discuss how drums can be used as a form of communication, then demonstrate a simple beat to represent the word *hello*. Ask students to follow your example with another word. Find this site on the Internet and share some of the folk tales with students.

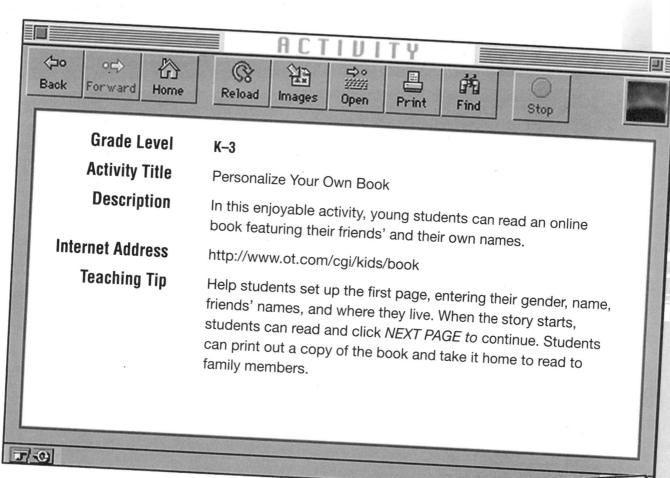

Grade Level	K–3
Activity Title	Personalize Your Own Book
Description	In this enjoyable activity, young students can read an online book featuring their friends' and their own names.
Internet Address	http://www.ot.com/cgi/kids/book
Teaching Tip	Help students set up the first page, entering their gender, name, friends' names, and where they live. When the story starts, students can read and click *NEXT PAGE to* continue. Students can print out a copy of the book and take it home to read to family members.

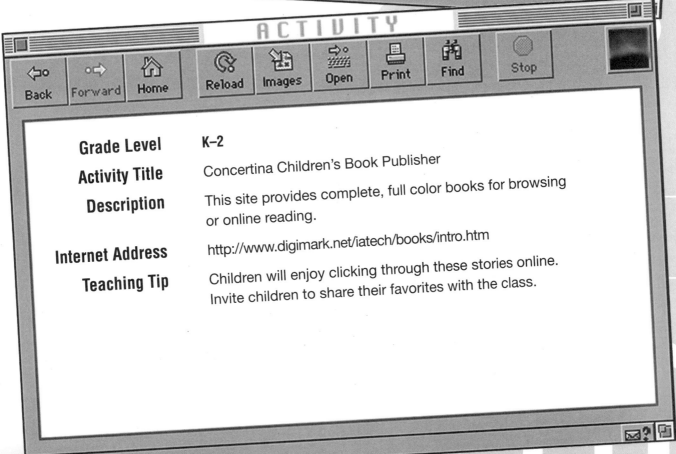

Grade Level	K–2
Activity Title	Concertina Children's Book Publisher
Description	This site provides complete, full color books for browsing or online reading.
Internet Address	http://www.digimark.net/iatech/books/intro.htm
Teaching Tip	Children will enjoy clicking through these stories online. Invite children to share their favorites with the class.

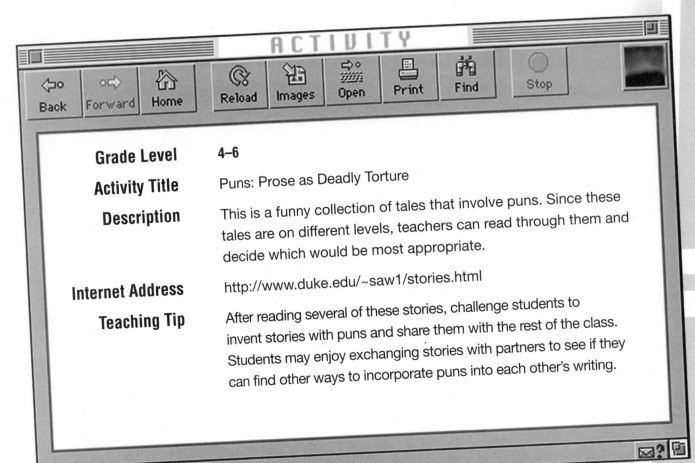

Back | Forward | Home | Reload | Images | Open | Print | Find | Stop

Grade Level	4–6
Activity Title	Puns: Prose as Deadly Torture
Description	This is a funny collection of tales that involve puns. Since these tales are on different levels, teachers can read through them and decide which would be most appropriate.
Internet Address	http://www.duke.edu/~saw1/stories.html
Teaching Tip	After reading several of these stories, challenge students to invent stories with puns and share them with the rest of the class. Students may enjoy exchanging stories with partners to see if they can find other ways to incorporate puns into each other's writing.

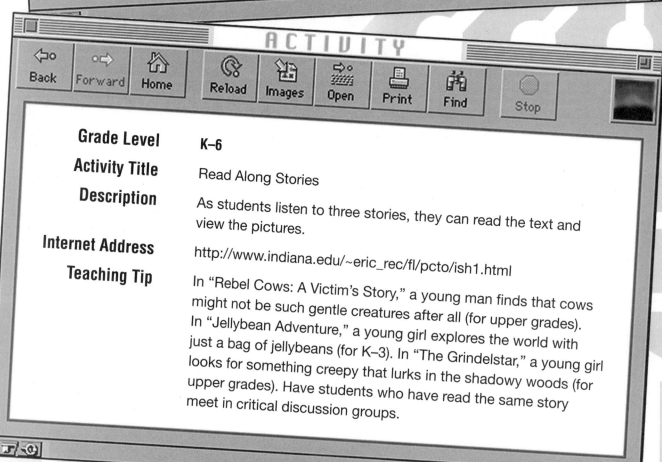

Back | Forward | Home | Reload | Images | Open | Print | Find | Stop

Grade Level	K–6
Activity Title	Read Along Stories
Description	As students listen to three stories, they can read the text and view the pictures.
Internet Address	http://www.indiana.edu/~eric_rec/fl/pcto/ish1.html
Teaching Tip	In "Rebel Cows: A Victim's Story," a young man finds that cows might not be such gentle creatures after all (for upper grades). In "Jellybean Adventure," a young girl explores the world with just a bag of jellybeans (for K–3). In "The Grindelstar," a young girl looks for something creepy that lurks in the shadowy woods (for upper grades). Have students who have read the same story meet in critical discussion groups.

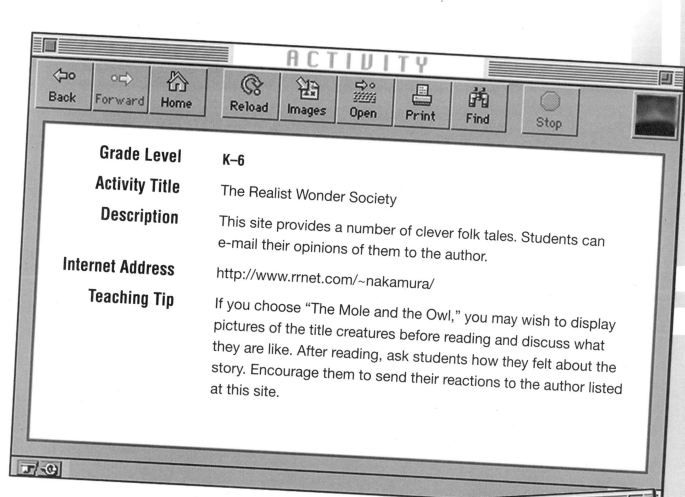

Grade Level	K–6
Activity Title	The Realist Wonder Society
Description	This site provides a number of clever folk tales. Students can e-mail their opinions of them to the author.
Internet Address	http://www.rrnet.com/~nakamura/
Teaching Tip	If you choose "The Mole and the Owl," you may wish to display pictures of the title creatures before reading and discuss what they are like. After reading, ask students how they felt about the story. Encourage them to send their reactions to the author listed at this site.

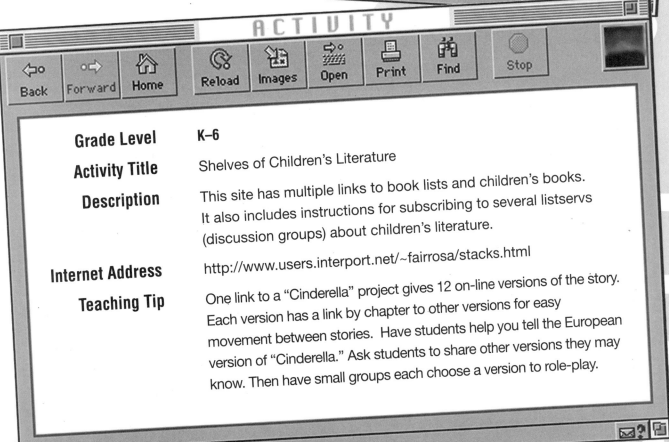

Grade Level	K–6
Activity Title	Shelves of Children's Literature
Description	This site has multiple links to book lists and children's books. It also includes instructions for subscribing to several listservs (discussion groups) about children's literature.
Internet Address	http://www.users.interport.net/~fairrosa/stacks.html
Teaching Tip	One link to a "Cinderella" project gives 12 on-line versions of the story. Each version has a link by chapter to other versions for easy movement between stories. Have students help you tell the European version of "Cinderella." Ask students to share other versions they may know. Then have small groups each choose a version to role-play.

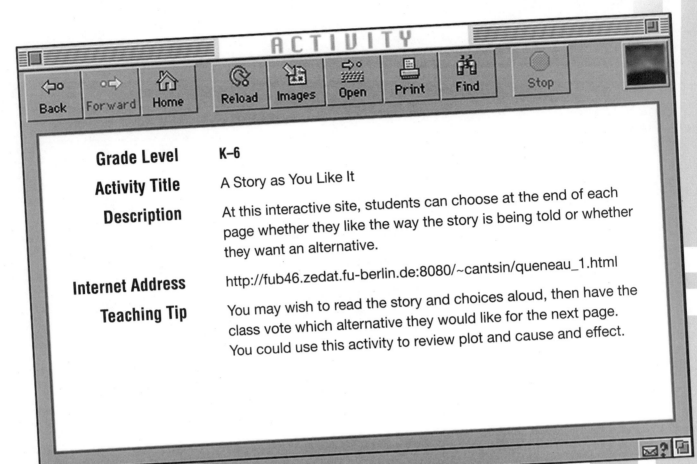

Back Forward Home Reload Images Open Print Find Stop

Grade Level K–6

Activity Title A Story as You Like It

Description At this interactive site, students can choose at the end of each page whether they like the way the story is being told or whether they want an alternative.

Internet Address http://fub46.zedat.fu-berlin.de:8080/~cantsin/queneau_1.html

Teaching Tip You may wish to read the story and choices aloud, then have the class vote which alternative they would like for the next page. You could use this activity to review plot and cause and effect.

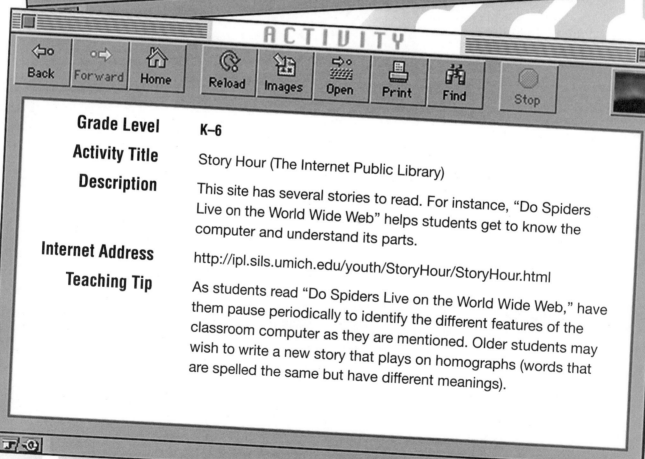

Back Forward Home Reload Images Open Print Find Stop

Grade Level K–6

Activity Title Story Hour (The Internet Public Library)

Description This site has several stories to read. For instance, "Do Spiders Live on the World Wide Web" helps students get to know the computer and understand its parts.

Internet Address http://ipl.sils.umich.edu/youth/StoryHour/StoryHour.html

Teaching Tip As students read "Do Spiders Live on the World Wide Web," have them pause periodically to identify the different features of the classroom computer as they are mentioned. Older students may wish to write a new story that plays on homographs (words that are spelled the same but have different meanings).

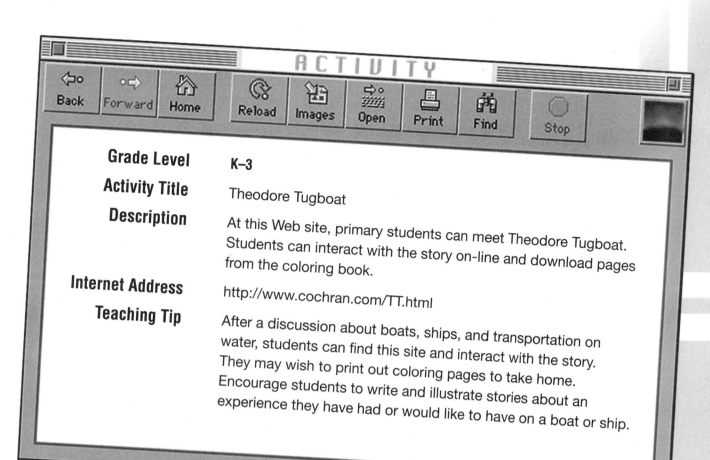

ACTIVITY

Grade Level	K–3
Activity Title	Theodore Tugboat
Description	At this Web site, primary students can meet Theodore Tugboat. Students can interact with the story on-line and download pages from the coloring book.
Internet Address	http://www.cochran.com/TT.html
Teaching Tip	After a discussion about boats, ships, and transportation on water, students can find this site and interact with the story. They may wish to print out coloring pages to take home. Encourage students to write and illustrate stories about an experience they have had or would like to have on a boat or ship.

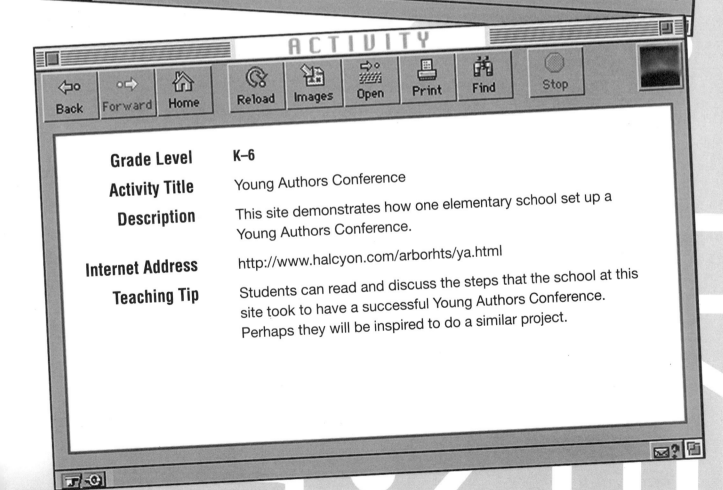

ACTIVITY

Grade Level	K–6
Activity Title	Young Authors Conference
Description	This site demonstrates how one elementary school set up a Young Authors Conference.
Internet Address	http://www.halcyon.com/arborhts/ya.html
Teaching Tip	Students can read and discuss the steps that the school at this site took to have a successful Young Authors Conference. Perhaps they will be inspired to do a similar project.

Chapter 7
Language Arts

This chapter describes a number of the most beneficial and enjoyable language arts resources for K–6 teachers to use, which include writing, spelling, and literature.

Language Arts Resources	K	1	2	3	4	5	6
Children's Illustrators on the Web	*	*	*	*	*	*	*
CNN-Interactive News					*	*	*
Crambo	*	*	*	*	*	*	*
Create Your Own Newspaper					*	*	*
CyberKids Interactive	*	*	*	*	*	*	*
Ernie's Learn [sic] to Speak a Little Hawaiian	*	*	*	*	*	*	*
The Gates of No Return					*	*	*
Haiku					*	*	*
Human Languages Page	*	*	*	*	*	*	*
The Internet Public Library	*	*	*	*	*	*	*
KID PUB	*	*	*	*	*	*	*
KIDSCOM			*	*	*	*	*
Sign Language and Braille	*	*	*	*	*	*	*
Webster's Dictionary	*	*	*	*	*	*	*
Welcome to the Labyrinth					*	*	*
Word by Word					*	*	*
Writers' Resources on the Web	*	*	*	*	*	*	*
Ziggy Piggy	*	*	*	*	*	*	*
	K	1	2	3	4	5	6

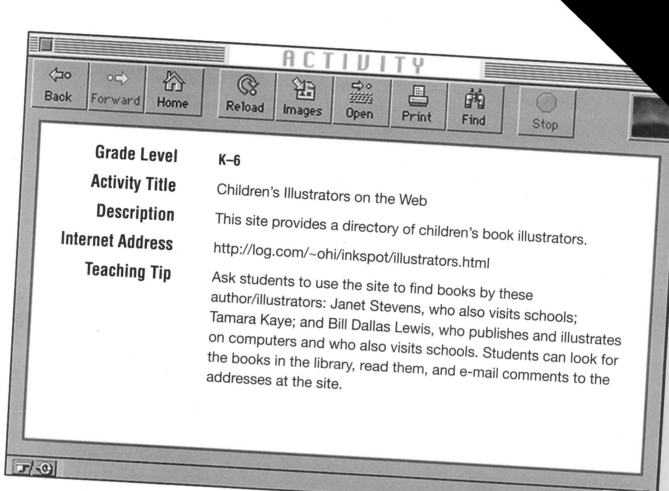

Back Forward Home Reload Images Open Print Find Stop

Grade Level K–6

Activity Title Children's Illustrators on the Web

Description This site provides a directory of children's book illustrators.

Internet Address http://log.com/~ohi/inkspot/illustrators.html

Teaching Tip Ask students to use the site to find books by these author/illustrators: Janet Stevens, who also visits schools; Tamara Kaye; and Bill Dallas Lewis, who publishes and illustrates on computers and who also visits schools. Students can look for the books in the library, read them, and e-mail comments to the addresses at the site.

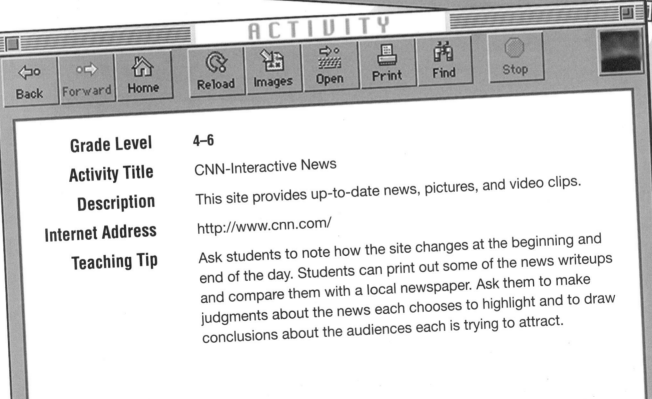

Back Forward Home Reload Images Open Print Find Stop

Grade Level 4–6

Activity Title CNN-Interactive News

Description This site provides up-to-date news, pictures, and video clips.

Internet Address http://www.cnn.com/

Teaching Tip Ask students to note how the site changes at the beginning and end of the day. Students can print out some of the news writeups and compare them with a local newspaper. Ask them to make judgments about the news each chooses to highlight and to draw conclusions about the audiences each is trying to attract.

Grade Level	K–6
Activity Title	Crambo
Description	This game helps students create rhyming phrases.
Internet Address	http://www.primenet.com/~hodges/kids_crambo.html
Teaching Tip	Allow students to play with some of the phrases at this site. Then they can play the game in pairs, groups, or teams.

Grade Level	4–6
Activity Title	Create Your Own Newspaper
Description	Students can use this site to create a personalized newspaper. It contains sample newspapers created with this program, news links (such as *TIME Daily News Summary* and *Today at NASA*), and daily statistics.
Internet Address	http://leeca8.leeca.ohio.gov/ofcs/ms/MTPV_Files/mtpv.html
Teaching Tip	Ask students to look at the sample newspapers at this site and decide which is their favorite format. Invite interested students to work in small groups to make a newspaper. They can use news sources provided at the site and add articles about their class or school. After the newspapers are ready, groups can distribute them and answer questions about their contents.

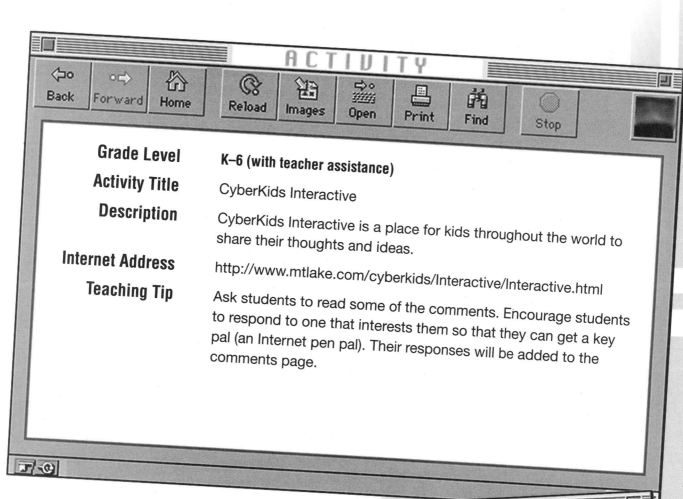

Back | Forward | Home | Reload | Images | Open | Print | Find | Stop

Grade Level — K–6 (with teacher assistance)

Activity Title — CyberKids Interactive

Description — CyberKids Interactive is a place for kids throughout the world to share their thoughts and ideas.

Internet Address — http://www.mtlake.com/cyberkids/Interactive/Interactive.html

Teaching Tip — Ask students to read some of the comments. Encourage students to respond to one that interests them so that they can get a key pal (an Internet pen pal). Their responses will be added to the comments page.

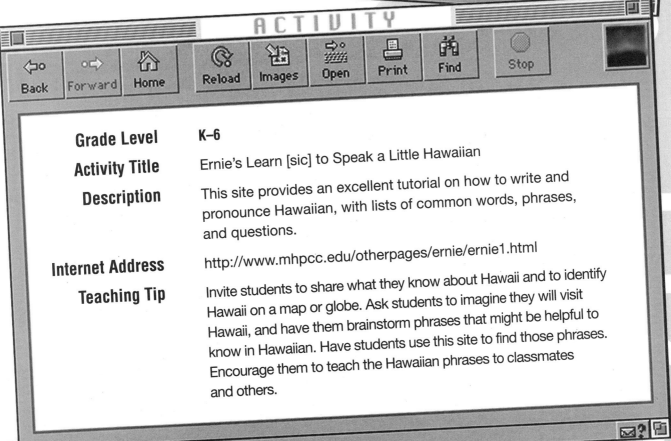

Back | Forward | Home | Reload | Images | Open | Print | Find | Stop

Grade Level — K–6

Activity Title — Ernie's Learn [sic] to Speak a Little Hawaiian

Description — This site provides an excellent tutorial on how to write and pronounce Hawaiian, with lists of common words, phrases, and questions.

Internet Address — http://www.mhpcc.edu/otherpages/ernie/ernie1.html

Teaching Tip — Invite students to share what they know about Hawaii and to identify Hawaii on a map or globe. Ask students to imagine they will visit Hawaii, and have them brainstorm phrases that might be helpful to know in Hawaiian. Have students use this site to find those phrases. Encourage them to teach the Hawaiian phrases to classmates and others.

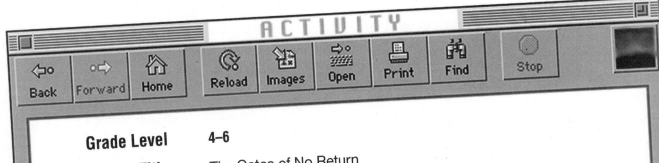

Back | Forward | Home | Reload | Images | Open | Print | Find | Stop

Grade Level 4–6

Activity Title The Gates of No Return

Description Students can read segments and choose different outcomes of this open-ended story. Once a direction is chosen, the student can add another segment.

Internet Address http://www.internet-for-kids.com/gate0.html

Teaching Tip Ask students to locate this site and take turns adding to the story. Have them compare outcomes and reasons for choosing them. Students might wish to create a new interactive story, adding it to your school's home page, if available, or sending it throughout the school.

Back | Forward | Home | Reload | Images | Open | Print | Find | Stop

Grade Level 4–6

Activity Title Haiku

Description These sites help people learn to compose and understand haiku, a form of poetry that originated in Japan.

Internet Addresses http://mikan.cc.matsuyama-u.ac.jp:80/~shiki/
http://www.oslonett.no/home/keitoy/haiku.html#howtowritehaiku

Teaching Tip Ask students to find either site and explore writing and understanding haiku. Initiate a discussion about haiku poems. Ask how the poems make students feel and how they would explain haiku to someone who has never heard of it before. Have students write and illustrate haiku poems and display them in the classroom.

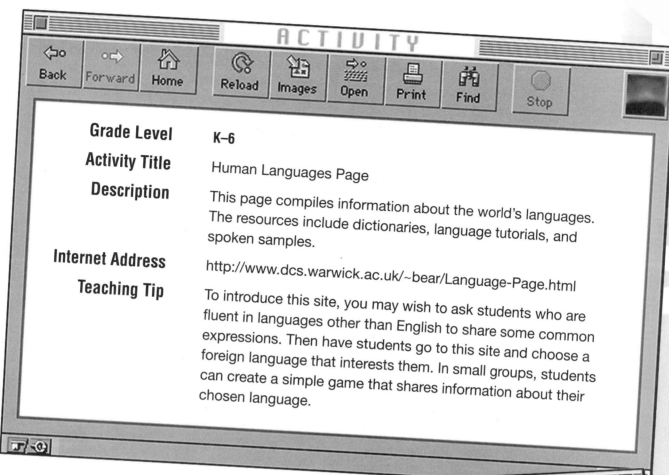

Grade Level K–6

Activity Title Human Languages Page

Description This page compiles information about the world's languages. The resources include dictionaries, language tutorials, and spoken samples.

Internet Address http://www.dcs.warwick.ac.uk/~bear/Language-Page.html

Teaching Tip To introduce this site, you may wish to ask students who are fluent in languages other than English to share some common expressions. Then have students go to this site and choose a foreign language that interests them. In small groups, students can create a simple game that shares information about their chosen language.

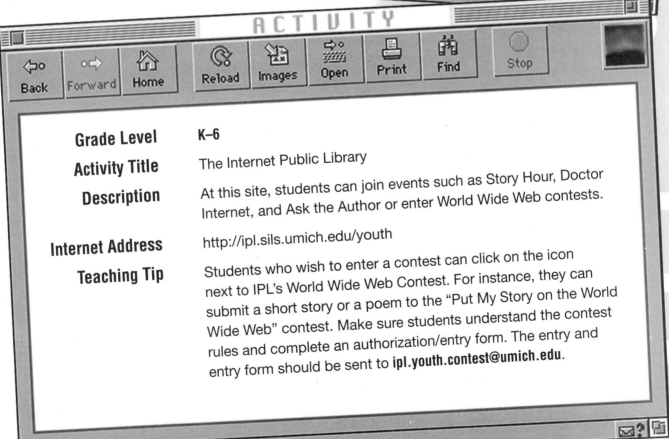

Grade Level K–6

Activity Title The Internet Public Library

Description At this site, students can join events such as Story Hour, Doctor Internet, and Ask the Author or enter World Wide Web contests.

Internet Address http://ipl.sils.umich.edu/youth

Teaching Tip Students who wish to enter a contest can click on the icon next to IPL's World Wide Web Contest. For instance, they can submit a short story or a poem to the "Put My Story on the World Wide Web" contest. Make sure students understand the contest rules and complete an authorization/entry form. The entry and entry form should be sent to **ipl.youth.contest@umich.edu**.

Grade Level   K–6

Activity Title   KID PUB

Description   At this site, students can write stories and get them published on-line. They can also read stories by other students.

Internet Address   http://en-garde.com/kidpub/

Teaching Tip   Students can write individual, group, or class stories and e-mail them to the address at this site. They can also look up the statistics section, which shows the number of stories the site receives each day, and view a chart showing where the stories come from.

ACTIVITY

Grade Level   2–6

Activity Title   KIDSCOM

Description   This site lets students ages 8–14 register for key pals with students throughout the world who share their interests.

Internet Address   http://www.kidscom.com

Teaching Tip   Ask students to list their favorite hobbies, books, movies, sports, and musical activities. Invite them to register with KIDSCOM, using their lists to help them find a key pal. They can communicate with their new friends via e-mail.

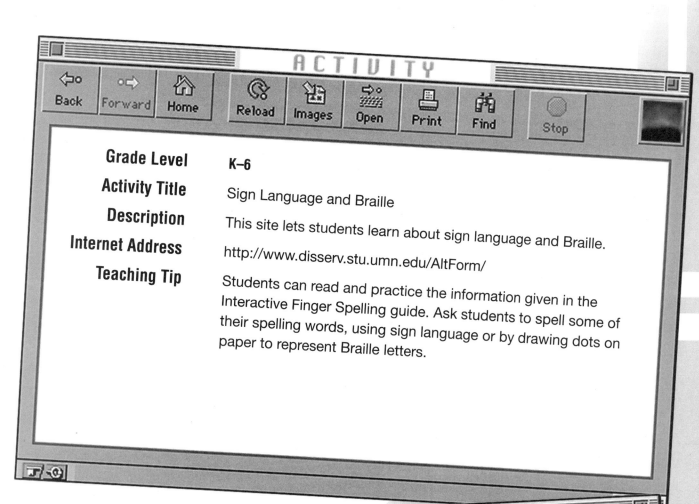

ACTIVITY

Grade Level	**K–6**
Activity Title	Sign Language and Braille
Description	This site lets students learn about sign language and Braille.
Internet Address	http://www.disserv.stu.umn.edu/AltForm/
Teaching Tip	Students can read and practice the information given in the Interactive Finger Spelling guide. Ask students to spell some of their spelling words, using sign language or by drawing dots on paper to represent Braille letters.

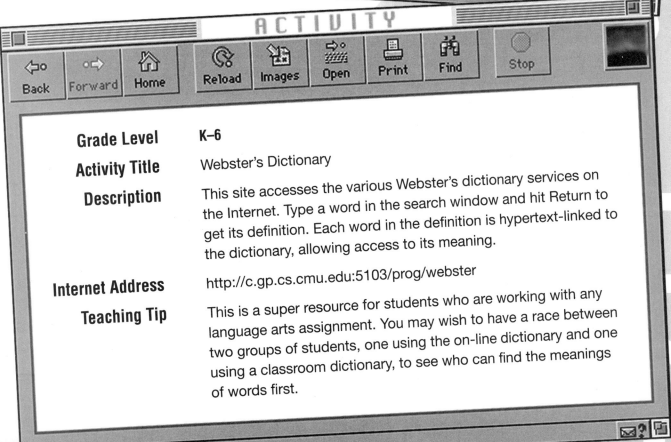

ACTIVITY

Grade Level	**K–6**
Activity Title	Webster's Dictionary
Description	This site accesses the various Webster's dictionary services on the Internet. Type a word in the search window and hit Return to get its definition. Each word in the definition is hypertext-linked to the dictionary, allowing access to its meaning.
Internet Address	http://c.gp.cs.cmu.edu:5103/prog/webster
Teaching Tip	This is a super resource for students who are working with any language arts assignment. You may wish to have a race between two groups of students, one using the on-line dictionary and one using a classroom dictionary, to see who can find the meanings of words first.

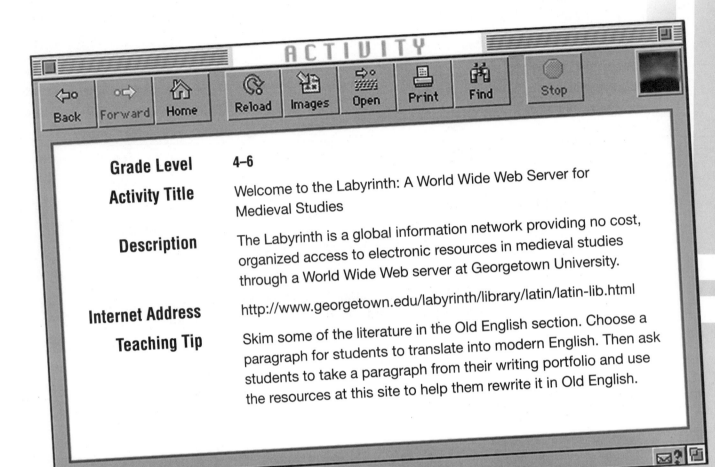

Grade Level	4–6
Activity Title	Welcome to the Labyrinth: A World Wide Web Server for Medieval Studies
Description	The Labyrinth is a global information network providing no cost, organized access to electronic resources in medieval studies through a World Wide Web server at Georgetown University.
Internet Address	http://www.georgetown.edu/labyrinth/library/latin/latin-lib.html
Teaching Tip	Skim some of the literature in the Old English section. Choose a paragraph for students to translate into modern English. Then ask students to take a paragraph from their writing portfolio and use the resources at this site to help them rewrite it in Old English.

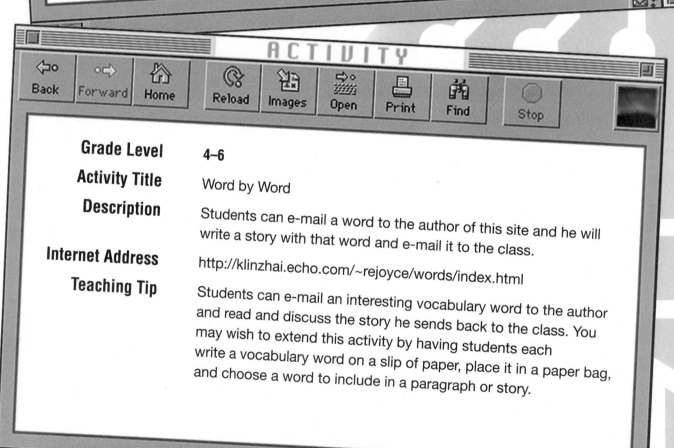

Grade Level	4–6
Activity Title	Word by Word
Description	Students can e-mail a word to the author of this site and he will write a story with that word and e-mail it to the class.
Internet Address	http://klinzhai.echo.com/~rejoyce/words/index.html
Teaching Tip	Students can e-mail an interesting vocabulary word to the author and read and discuss the story he sends back to the class. You may wish to extend this activity by having students each write a vocabulary word on a slip of paper, place it in a paper bag, and choose a word to include in a paragraph or story.

ACTIVITY

Treasure Chest Site!

| Back | Forward | Home | Reload | Images | Open | Print | Find |

Grade Level   K–6

Activity Title   Writers' Resources on the Web

Description

Topics include children's writing, science fiction/fantasy, mystery, poetry, journalism, technical/scientific writing, and travel writing. There is a reference library with authors, illustrators, awards, search tools, online literature, and publications. For young writers there are contests, workshops, and more.

Internet Address   http://interlog.com/~ohi/www/writesource.html

Teaching Tip

This site provides a quick and easy resource of different writing styles. After looking at the genres, students can take a story they've written and change it into a mystery or science fiction tale. Students may wish to enter story contests at this site.

ACTIVITY

| Back | Forward | Home | Reload | Images | Open | Print | Find | Stop |

Grade Level   K–6

Activity Title   Ziggy Piggy

Description

This fun and silly rhyming game will help students develop logical reasoning.

Internet Address   http://www.primenet.com/~hodges/kids_crambo.html

Teaching Tip

Have students investigate some of the problems at this site. Then encourage them to think of more. Ask small groups to write and illustrate a book based on "ziggy piggy" phrases. Before they start, provide this example: *The soggy froggy went for a walk.*

Language Arts   79

Chapter 8
Math

This chapter contains a number of the most beneficial and enjoyable math resources for K–6 teachers to use. This area includes problem solving, logical reasoning, and math skills.

Math Resources	K	1	2	3	4	5	6
Ask Dr. Math					*	*	*
Bluedog Can Count!			*	*	*	*	*
Connect Four			*	*	*	*	*
Cute Number Facts: About Today's Date			*	*	*	*	*
The Electronic Zoo: Animal Resources	*	*	*	*	*	*	*
Fastball	*	*	*	*	*	*	*
Film Canister Kaleidoscope					*	*	*
Fun Math					*	*	*
The Geometry Forum					*	*	*
The Great Penny Toss	*	*	*	*	*	*	*
Hands on the Giant	*	*	*	*	*	*	*
How Money Is Made	*	*	*	*	*	*	*
Mapmaker, Mapmaker, Make Me a Map			*	*	*	*	*
Mathematics	*	*	*	*	*	*	*
Math Magic	*	*	*	*	*	*	*
Population World Counter					*	*	*
Spirographs and Math!	*	*	*	*	*	*	*
Street Cents					*	*	*
Teaching and Learning About Chess					*	*	*
Team-by-Team Statistics					*	*	*
The World of Escher					*	*	*
	K	1	2	3	4	5	6

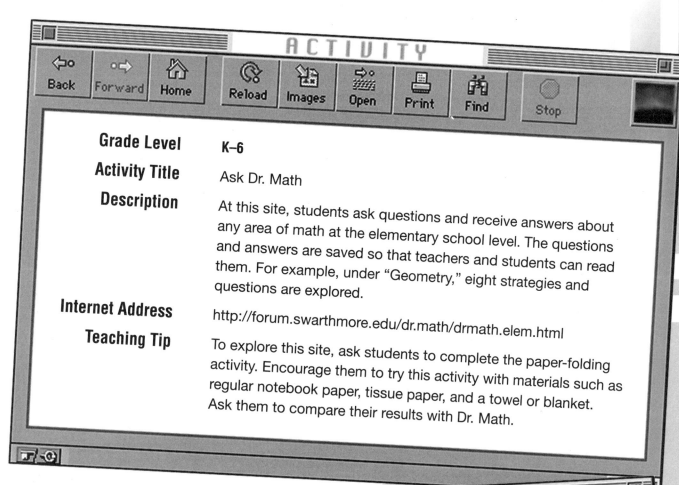

Grade Level K–6

Activity Title Ask Dr. Math

Description At this site, students ask questions and receive answers about any area of math at the elementary school level. The questions and answers are saved so that teachers and students can read them. For example, under "Geometry," eight strategies and questions are explored.

Internet Address http://forum.swarthmore.edu/dr.math/drmath.elem.html

Teaching Tip To explore this site, ask students to complete the paper-folding activity. Encourage them to try this activity with materials such as regular notebook paper, tissue paper, and a towel or blanket. Ask them to compare their results with Dr. Math.

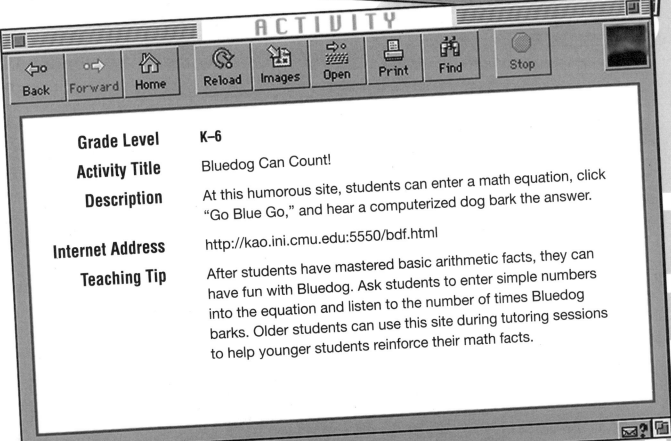

Grade Level K–6

Activity Title Bluedog Can Count!

Description At this humorous site, students can enter a math equation, click "Go Blue Go," and hear a computerized dog bark the answer.

Internet Address http://kao.ini.cmu.edu:5550/bdf.html

Teaching Tip After students have mastered basic arithmetic facts, they can have fun with Bluedog. Ask students to enter simple numbers into the equation and listen to the number of times Bluedog barks. Older students can use this site during tutoring sessions to help younger students reinforce their math facts.

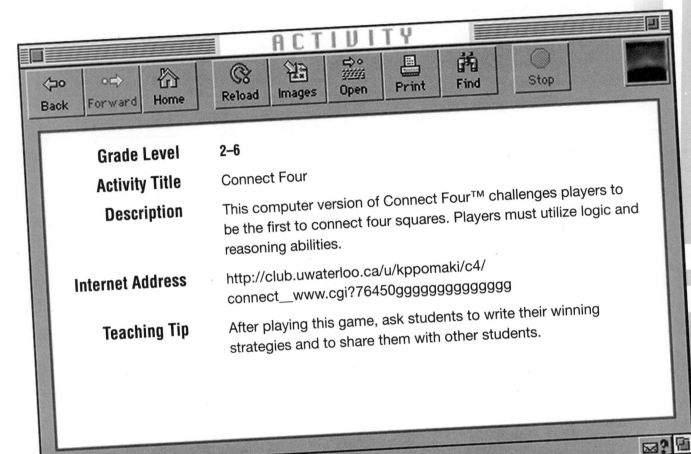

Grade Level   2–6

Activity Title   Connect Four

Description   This computer version of Connect Four™ challenges players to be the first to connect four squares. Players must utilize logic and reasoning abilities.

Internet Address   http://club.uwaterloo.ca/u/kppomaki/c4/ connect__www.cgi?76450gggggggggggggg

Teaching Tip   After playing this game, ask students to write their winning strategies and to share them with other students.

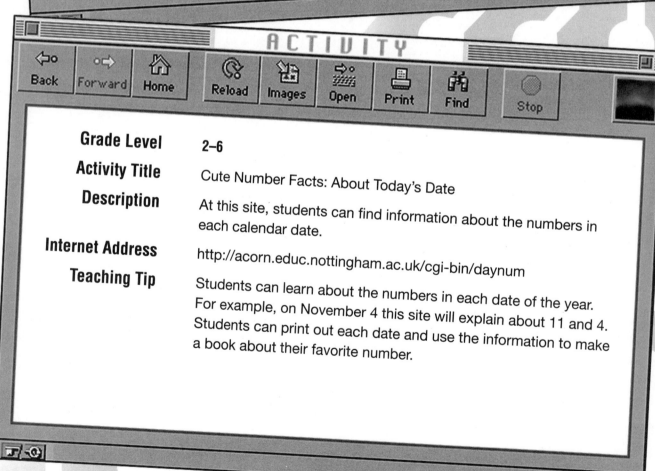

Grade Level   2–6

Activity Title   Cute Number Facts: About Today's Date

Description   At this site, students can find information about the numbers in each calendar date.

Internet Address   http://acorn.educ.nottingham.ac.uk/cgi-bin/daynum

Teaching Tip   Students can learn about the numbers in each date of the year. For example, on November 4 this site will explain about 11 and 4. Students can print out each date and use the information to make a book about their favorite number.

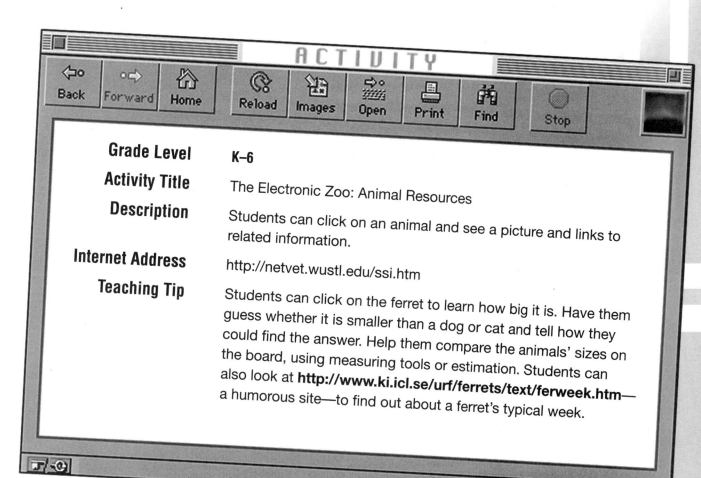

Back	Forward	Home	Reload	Images	Open	Print	Find	Stop

Grade Level   K–6

Activity Title   The Electronic Zoo: Animal Resources

Description   Students can click on an animal and see a picture and links to related information.

Internet Address   http://netvet.wustl.edu/ssi.htm

Teaching Tip   Students can click on the ferret to learn how big it is. Have them guess whether it is smaller than a dog or cat and tell how they could find the answer. Help them compare the animals' sizes on the board, using measuring tools or estimation. Students can also look at **http://www.ki.icl.se/urf/ferrets/text/ferweek.htm**— a humorous site—to find out about a ferret's typical week.

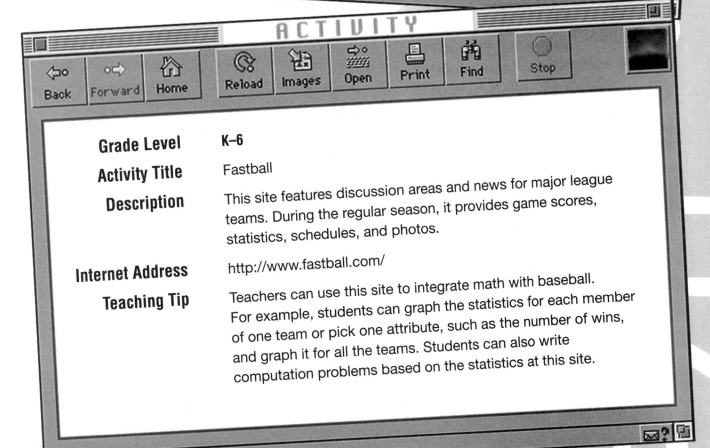

Back	Forward	Home	Reload	Images	Open	Print	Find	Stop

Grade Level   K–6

Activity Title   Fastball

Description   This site features discussion areas and news for major league teams. During the regular season, it provides game scores, statistics, schedules, and photos.

Internet Address   http://www.fastball.com/

Teaching Tip   Teachers can use this site to integrate math with baseball. For example, students can graph the statistics for each member of one team or pick one attribute, such as the number of wins, and graph it for all the teams. Students can also write computation problems based on the statistics at this site.

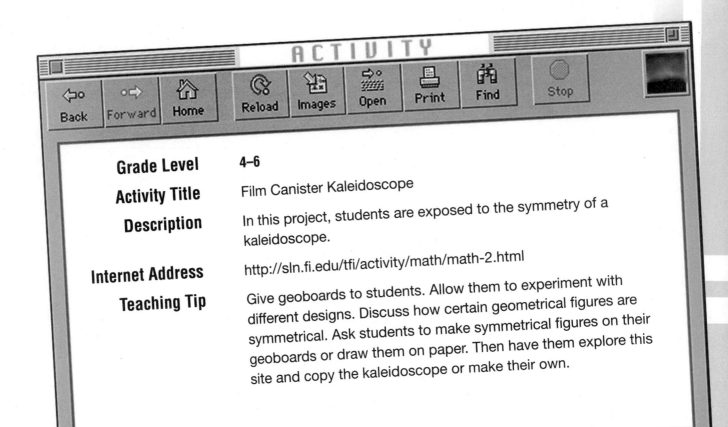

Back | Forward | Home | Reload | Images | Open | Print | Find | Stop

Grade Level   4–6

Activity Title   Film Canister Kaleidoscope

Description   In this project, students are exposed to the symmetry of a kaleidoscope.

Internet Address   http://sln.fi.edu/tfi/activity/math/math-2.html

Teaching Tip   Give geoboards to students. Allow them to experiment with different designs. Discuss how certain geometrical figures are symmetrical. Ask students to make symmetrical figures on their geoboards or draw them on paper. Then have them explore this site and copy the kaleidoscope or make their own.

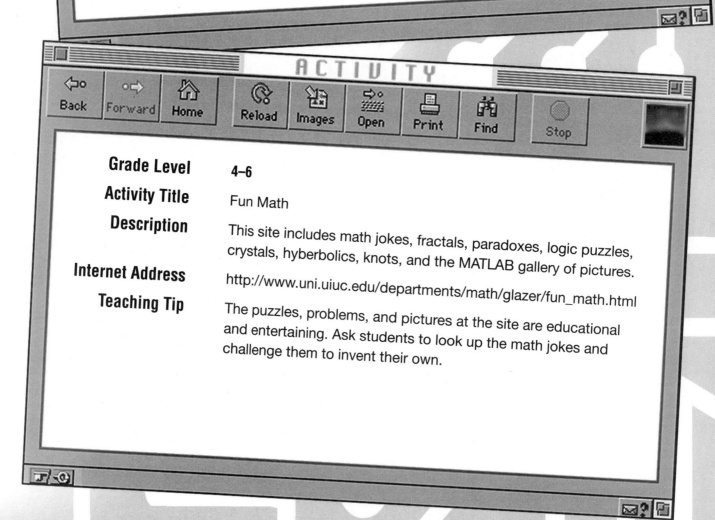

Back | Forward | Home | Reload | Images | Open | Print | Find | Stop

Grade Level   4–6

Activity Title   Fun Math

Description   This site includes math jokes, fractals, paradoxes, logic puzzles, crystals, hyberbolics, knots, and the MATLAB gallery of pictures.

Internet Address   http://www.uni.uiuc.edu/departments/math/glazer/fun_math.html

Teaching Tip   The puzzles, problems, and pictures at the site are educational and entertaining. Ask students to look up the math jokes and challenge them to invent their own.

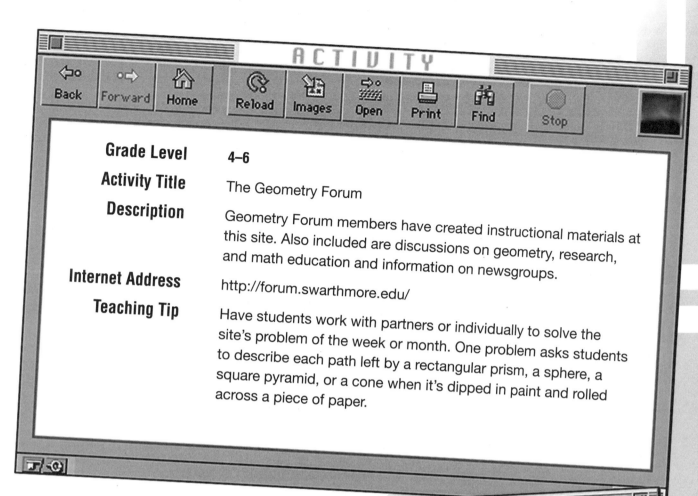

ACTIVITY

Back | Forward | Home | Reload | Images | Open | Print | Find | Stop

Grade Level	4–6
Activity Title	The Geometry Forum
Description	Geometry Forum members have created instructional materials at this site. Also included are discussions on geometry, research, and math education and information on newsgroups.
Internet Address	http://forum.swarthmore.edu/
Teaching Tip	Have students work with partners or individually to solve the site's problem of the week or month. One problem asks students to describe each path left by a rectangular prism, a sphere, a square pyramid, or a cone when it's dipped in paint and rolled across a piece of paper.

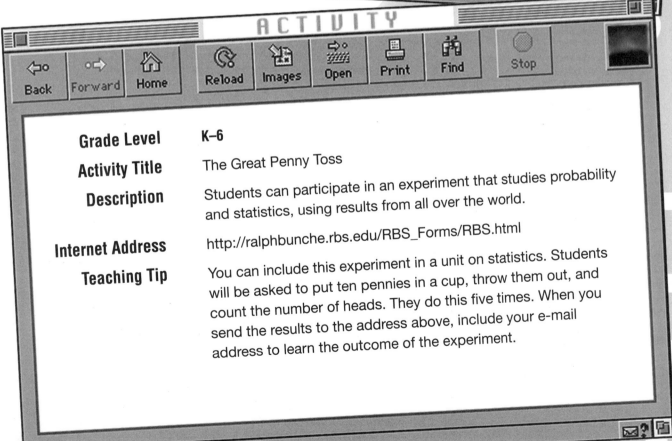

ACTIVITY

Back | Forward | Home | Reload | Images | Open | Print | Find | Stop

Grade Level	K–6
Activity Title	The Great Penny Toss
Description	Students can participate in an experiment that studies probability and statistics, using results from all over the world.
Internet Address	http://ralphbunche.rbs.edu/RBS_Forms/RBS.html
Teaching Tip	You can include this experiment in a unit on statistics. Students will be asked to put ten pennies in a cup, throw them out, and count the number of heads. They do this five times. When you send the results to the address above, include your e-mail address to learn the outcome of the experiment.

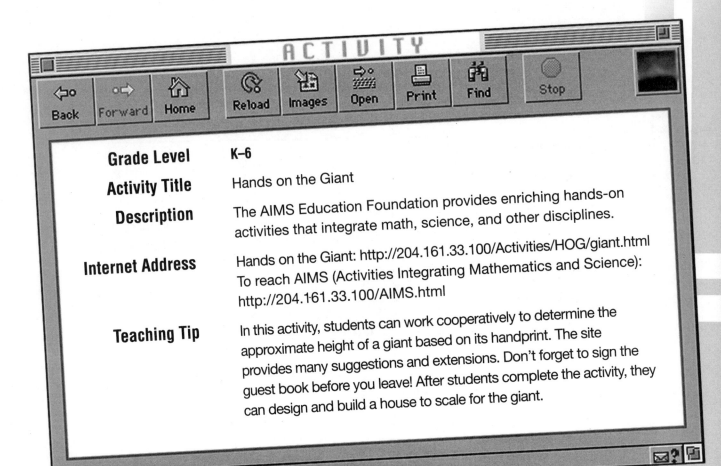

Grade Level	K–6
Activity Title	Hands on the Giant
Description	The AIMS Education Foundation provides enriching hands-on activities that integrate math, science, and other disciplines.
Internet Address	Hands on the Giant: http://204.161.33.100/Activities/HOG/giant.html To reach AIMS (Activities Integrating Mathematics and Science): http://204.161.33.100/AIMS.html
Teaching Tip	In this activity, students can work cooperatively to determine the approximate height of a giant based on its handprint. The site provides many suggestions and extensions. Don't forget to sign the guest book before you leave! After students complete the activity, they can design and build a house to scale for the giant.

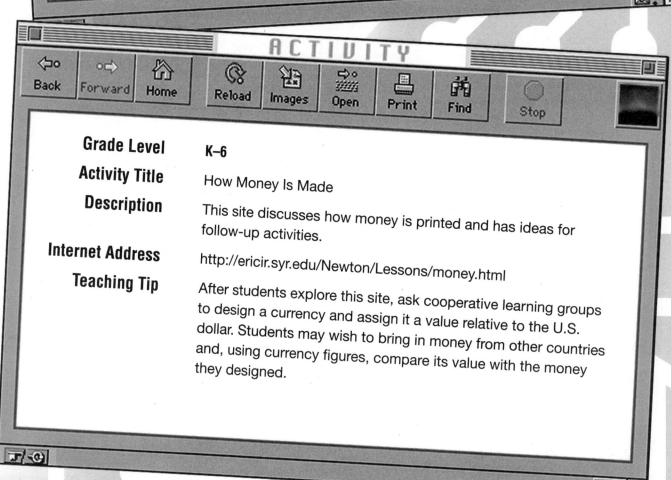

Grade Level	K–6
Activity Title	How Money Is Made
Description	This site discusses how money is printed and has ideas for follow-up activities.
Internet Address	http://ericir.syr.edu/Newton/Lessons/money.html
Teaching Tip	After students explore this site, ask cooperative learning groups to design a currency and assign it a value relative to the U.S. dollar. Students may wish to bring in money from other countries and, using currency figures, compare its value with the money they designed.

Grade Level	2–6
Activity Title	Mapmaker, Mapmaker, Make Me a Map
Description	This site contains ideas and information on mapmaking. Students can use the information to help them measure distances and plot longitude and latitude.
Internet Address	http://loki.ur.utk.edu/ut2kids/maps/map.html
Teaching Tip	Ask students to draw a map of their classroom. Younger children can estimate how many hands would fit lengthwise in the class. Older students can draw the room to scale. After students make maps, let them explore this Internet site.

Treasure Chest Site!

Grade Level	K–6
Activity Title	Mathematics
Description	This site contains thousands of activities and resources in general mathematics, problem solving and reasoning, mathematical tools, whole numbers and numeration, measurement, geometry, statistics and probability, and algebraic ideas.
Internet Address	http://unite.ukans.edu/Browser/UNITEResource/Layer_Mathematics.html
Teaching Tip	K–6 teachers can use this site every day. In problem solving and reasoning, for instance, you'll find more than 800 activities and resources. Some, such as "M&M's Chocolate Counting Book," are for younger children, and some, such as "Mayan Addition," are for older students.

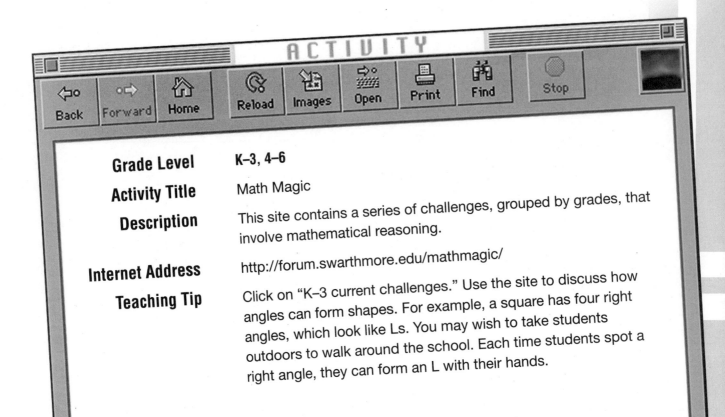

Grade Level   K–3, 4–6

Activity Title   Math Magic

Description   This site contains a series of challenges, grouped by grades, that involve mathematical reasoning.

Internet Address   http://forum.swarthmore.edu/mathmagic/

Teaching Tip   Click on "K–3 current challenges." Use the site to discuss how angles can form shapes. For example, a square has four right angles, which look like Ls. You may wish to take students outdoors to walk around the school. Each time students spot a right angle, they can form an L with their hands.

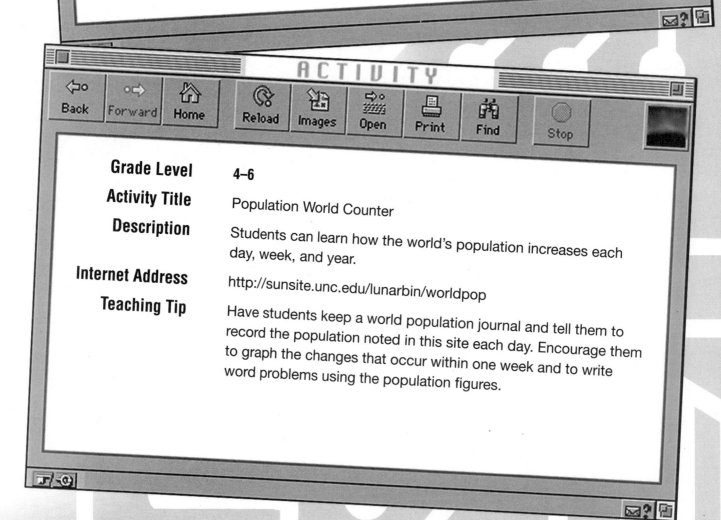

Grade Level   4–6

Activity Title   Population World Counter

Description   Students can learn how the world's population increases each day, week, and year.

Internet Address   http://sunsite.unc.edu/lunarbin/worldpop

Teaching Tip   Have students keep a world population journal and tell them to record the population noted in this site each day. Encourage them to graph the changes that occur within one week and to write word problems using the population figures.

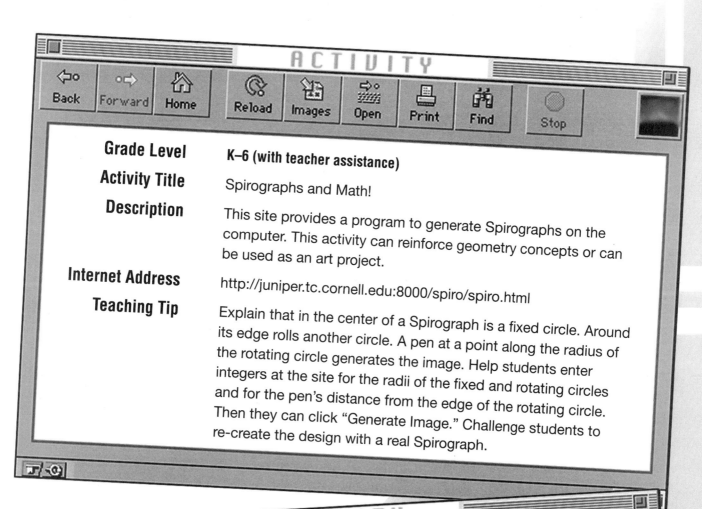

Grade Level	K–6 (with teacher assistance)
Activity Title	Spirographs and Math!
Description	This site provides a program to generate Spirographs on the computer. This activity can reinforce geometry concepts or can be used as an art project.
Internet Address	http://juniper.tc.cornell.edu:8000/spiro/spiro.html
Teaching Tip	Explain that in the center of a Spirograph is a fixed circle. Around its edge rolls another circle. A pen at a point along the radius of the rotating circle generates the image. Help students enter integers at the site for the radii of the fixed and rotating circles and for the pen's distance from the edge of the rotating circle. Then they can click "Generate Image." Challenge students to re-create the design with a real Spirograph.

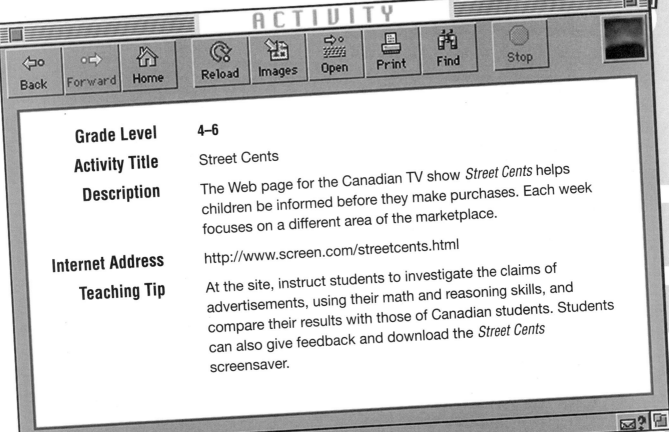

Grade Level	4–6
Activity Title	Street Cents
Description	The Web page for the Canadian TV show *Street Cents* helps children be informed before they make purchases. Each week focuses on a different area of the marketplace.
Internet Address	http://www.screen.com/streetcents.html
Teaching Tip	At the site, instruct students to investigate the claims of advertisements, using their math and reasoning skills, and compare their results with those of Canadian students. Students can also give feedback and download the *Street Cents* screensaver.

Back   Forward   Home   Reload   Images   Open   Print   Find   Stop

Grade Level	4–6
Activity Title	Teaching and Learning About Chess
Description	This site explores different aspects of chess.
Internet Address	http://info.ex.ac.uk/~dregis/DR/coaching.html
Teaching Tip	After students find the main Web site, they can click "Examples of Handouts," then click "Top 10 Tips for Juniors." This area provides advice for children who are learning to play chess. Provide students with chess sets so that they can try out the tips.

Back   Forward   Home   Reload   Images   Open   Print   Find   Stop

Grade Level	4–6
Activity Title	Team-by-Team Statistics
Description	This site provides information about NBA teams, including statistics on each team member.
Internet Address	http://espnet.sportszone.com/nba/
Teaching Tip	Ask students to look up their favorite team. Students could examine the statistics to determine such questions as *Who played the most minutes in your team?* Students could also graph the top three scorers and compare their results with those of other students.

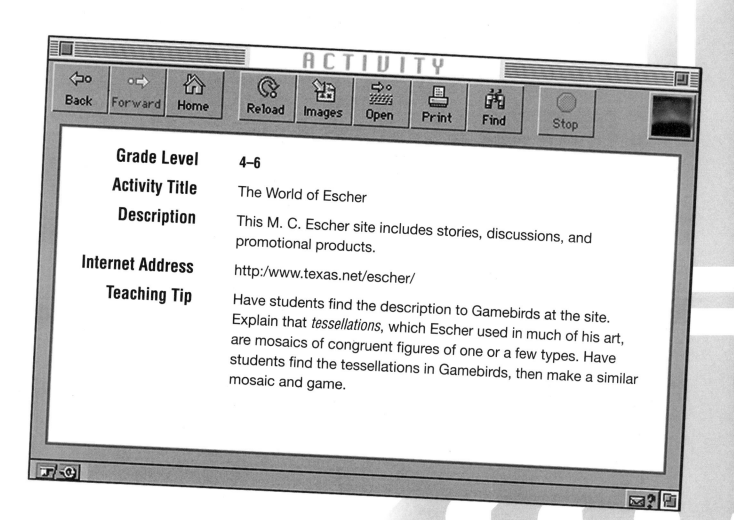

ACTIVITY

⇦o Back	o⇨ Forward	⌂ Home	Reload	Images	Open	Print	Find	Stop

Grade Level   4–6

Activity Title   The World of Escher

Description   This M. C. Escher site includes stories, discussions, and promotional products.

Internet Address   http:/www.texas.net/escher/

Teaching Tip   Have students find the description to Gamebirds at the site. Explain that *tessellations*, which Escher used in much of his art, are mosaics of congruent figures of one or a few types. Have students find the tessellations in Gamebirds, then make a similar mosaic and game.

Chapter 9
Science

In this chapter you will find a number of the most beneficial and enjoyable science resources for K–6 teachers. This area includes problem solving, developing the processes of science, and using the scientific method in practical applications.

Science Resources	K	1	2	3	4	5	6
All About Frogs	*	*	*	*	*	*	*
Ask-an-Astronomer	*	*	*	*	*	*	*
Astronomy Picture of the Day	*	*	*	*	*	*	*
Bird Calls	*	*	*	*	*	*	*
The Bug Club					*	*	*
Cells Alive!					*	*	*
Complete List of Dog-Related Web Sites	*	*	*	*	*	*	*
Dinosaur Hall					*	*	*
Florida Aquarium	*	*	*	*	*	*	*
The Global Schoolhouse Project					*	*	*
Kids-Weathernet	*	*	*	*	*	*	*
Mouse Trap Powered Vehicle Challenge!					*	*	*
Rain Forest: White Jag					*	*	*
Robot Web Page Menu	*	*	*	*	*	*	*
Science Gateway	*	*	*	*	*	*	*
View of the Solar System	*	*	*	*	*	*	*
Virtual Frog Dissection Kit, Version 1.2					*	*	*
Volcano World	*	*	*	*	*	*	*
Weather Underground: A Complete U.S. Weather Service					*	*	*
A Whale of a Tale: Whales	*	*	*	*	*	*	*
The Wind: Our Fierce Friend	*	*	*	*	*	*	*
Youngstown Freenet	*	*	*	*	*	*	*
	K	1	2	3	4	5	6

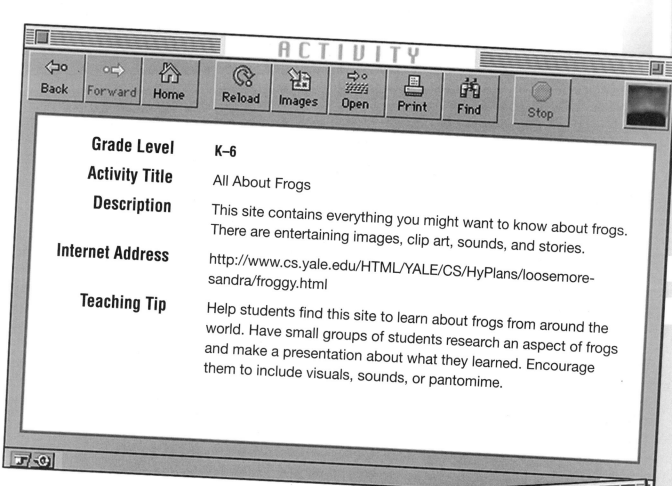

Back   Forward   Home   Reload   Images   Open   Print   Find   Stop

Grade Level   K–6

Activity Title   All About Frogs

Description   This site contains everything you might want to know about frogs. There are entertaining images, clip art, sounds, and stories.

Internet Address   http://www.cs.yale.edu/HTML/YALE/CS/HyPlans/loosemore-sandra/froggy.html

Teaching Tip   Help students find this site to learn about frogs from around the world. Have small groups of students research an aspect of frogs and make a presentation about what they learned. Encourage them to include visuals, sounds, or pantomime.

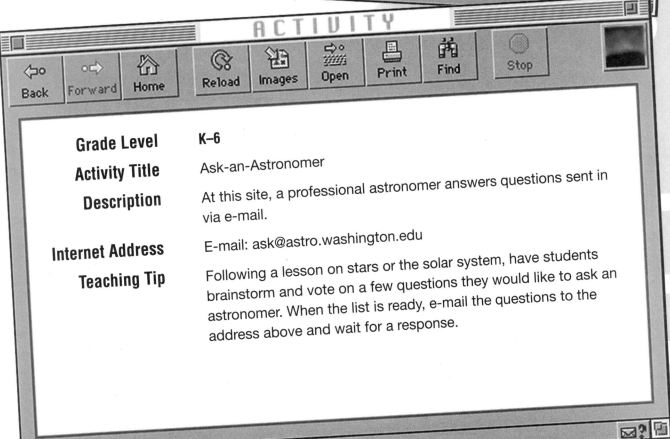

Back   Forward   Home   Reload   Images   Open   Print   Find   Stop

Grade Level   K–6

Activity Title   Ask-an-Astronomer

Description   At this site, a professional astronomer answers questions sent in via e-mail.

E-mail: ask@astro.washington.edu

Internet Address

Teaching Tip   Following a lesson on stars or the solar system, have students brainstorm and vote on a few questions they would like to ask an astronomer. When the list is ready, e-mail the questions to the address above and wait for a response.

Science   93

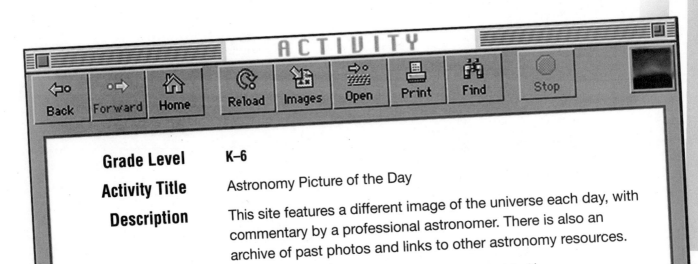

Grade Level   K–6

Activity Title   Astronomy Picture of the Day

Description   This site features a different image of the universe each day, with commentary by a professional astronomer. There is also an archive of past photos and links to other astronomy resources.

Internet Address   http://antwrp.gsfc.nasa.gov/apod/astropix.html/

Teaching Tip   After a field trip to a planetarium, this site can be used to review stars, planets, and constellations. Provide this site address to parents who have Internet access and encourage them to visit this site with their children at home. The photos may inspire families to see what they can find in the night sky.

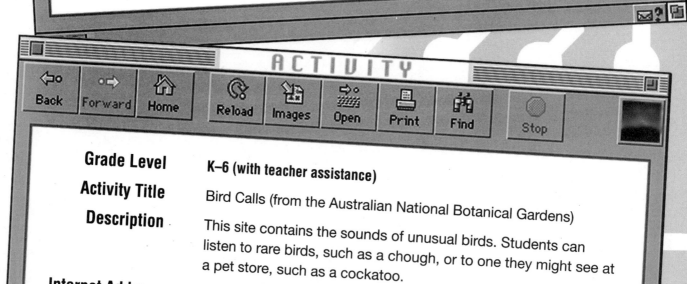

Grade Level   K–6 (with teacher assistance)

Activity Title   Bird Calls (from the Australian National Botanical Gardens)

Description   This site contains the sounds of unusual birds. Students can listen to rare birds, such as a chough, or to one they might see at a pet store, such as a cockatoo.

Internet Address   http://155.187.10.12:80/sounds/

Teaching Tip   At this site, students can tape-record several sounds and try to match sounds with birds. Challenge students to research one of the birds to find out what it looks like, where it lives, and what it is like.

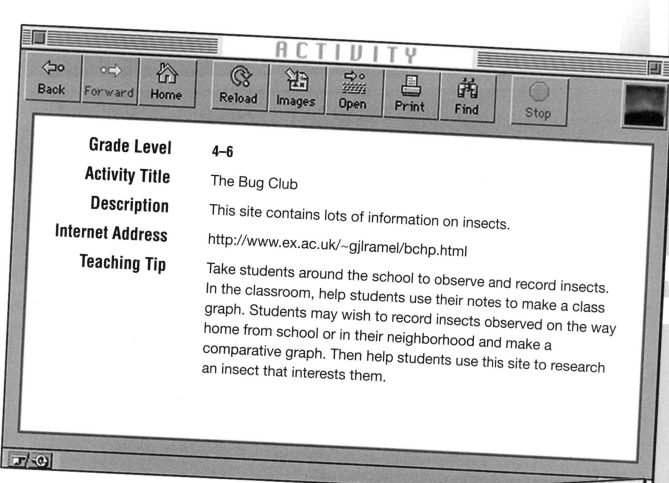

Back   Forward   Home   Reload   Images   Open   Print   Find   Stop

Grade Level   4–6

Activity Title   The Bug Club

Description   This site contains lots of information on insects.

Internet Address   http://www.ex.ac.uk/~gjlramel/bchp.html

Teaching Tip   Take students around the school to observe and record insects. In the classroom, help students use their notes to make a class graph. Students may wish to record insects observed on the way home from school or in their neighborhood and make a comparative graph. Then help students use this site to research an insect that interests them.

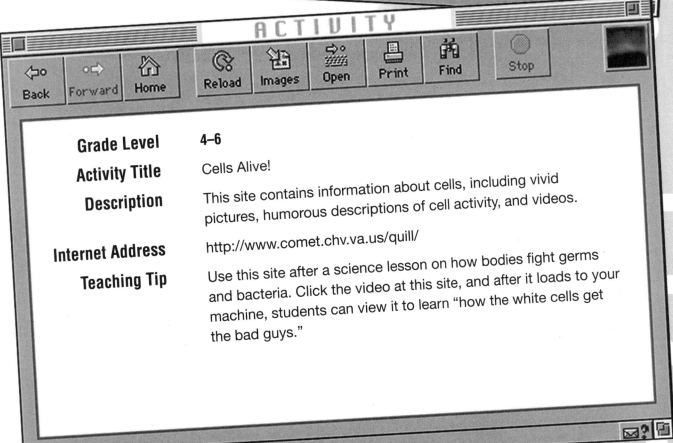

Back   Forward   Home   Reload   Images   Open   Print   Find   Stop

Grade Level   4–6

Activity Title   Cells Alive!

Description   This site contains information about cells, including vivid pictures, humorous descriptions of cell activity, and videos.

Internet Address   http://www.comet.chv.va.us/quill/

Teaching Tip   Use this site after a science lesson on how bodies fight germs and bacteria. Click the video at this site, and after it loads to your machine, students can view it to learn "how the white cells get the bad guys."

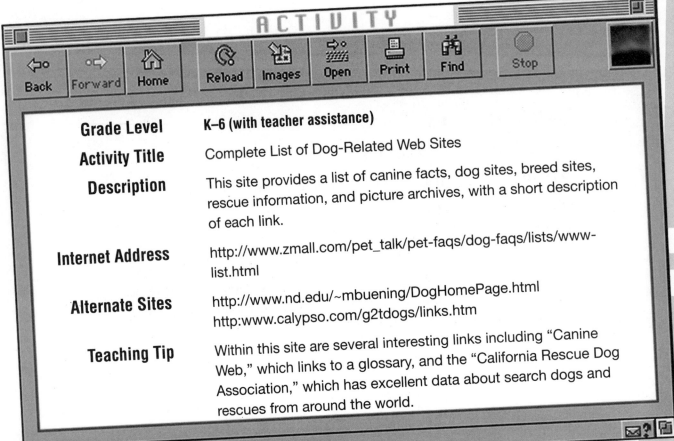

ACTIVITY

Grade Level	K–6 (with teacher assistance)
Activity Title	Complete List of Dog-Related Web Sites
Description	This site provides a list of canine facts, dog sites, breed sites, rescue information, and picture archives, with a short description of each link.
Internet Address	http://www.zmall.com/pet_talk/pet-faqs/dog-faqs/lists/www-list.html
Alternate Sites	http://www.nd.edu/~mbuening/DogHomePage.html http:www.calypso.com/g2tdogs/links.htm
Teaching Tip	Within this site are several interesting links including "Canine Web," which links to a glossary, and the "California Rescue Dog Association," which has excellent data about search dogs and rescues from around the world.

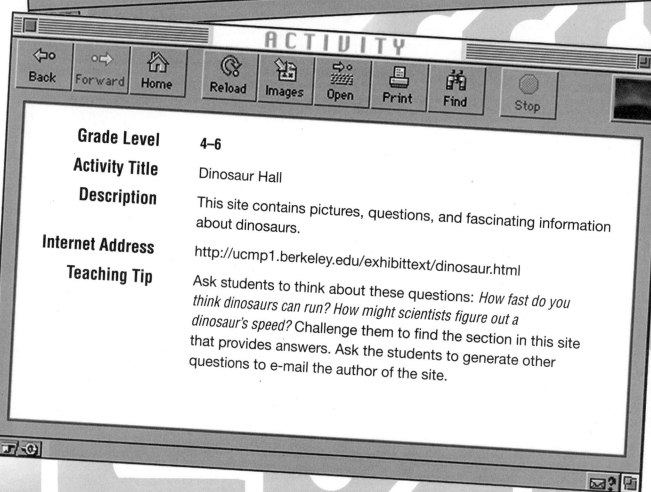

ACTIVITY

Grade Level	4–6
Activity Title	Dinosaur Hall
Description	This site contains pictures, questions, and fascinating information about dinosaurs.
Internet Address	http://ucmp1.berkeley.edu/exhibittext/dinosaur.html
Teaching Tip	Ask students to think about these questions: *How fast do you think dinosaurs can run? How might scientists figure out a dinosaur's speed?* Challenge them to find the section in this site that provides answers. Ask the students to generate other questions to e-mail the author of the site.

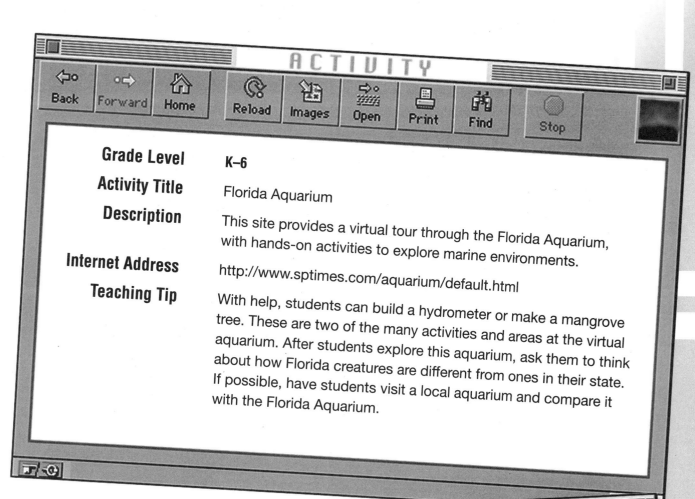

ACTIVITY

Grade Level	K–6
Activity Title	Florida Aquarium
Description	This site provides a virtual tour through the Florida Aquarium, with hands-on activities to explore marine environments.
Internet Address	http://www.sptimes.com/aquarium/default.html
Teaching Tip	With help, students can build a hydrometer or make a mangrove tree. These are two of the many activities and areas at the virtual aquarium. After students explore this aquarium, ask them to think about how Florida creatures are different from ones in their state. If possible, have students visit a local aquarium and compare it with the Florida Aquarium.

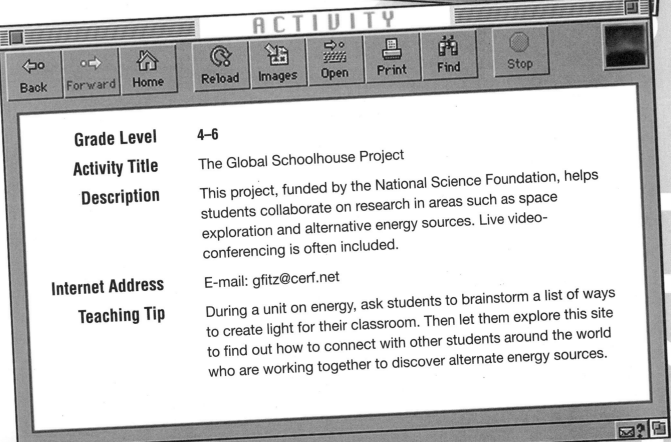

ACTIVITY

Grade Level	4–6
Activity Title	The Global Schoolhouse Project
Description	This project, funded by the National Science Foundation, helps students collaborate on research in areas such as space exploration and alternative energy sources. Live video-conferencing is often included.
Internet Address	E-mail: gfitz@cerf.net
Teaching Tip	During a unit on energy, ask students to brainstorm a list of ways to create light for their classroom. Then let them explore this site to find out how to connect with other students around the world who are working together to discover alternate energy sources.

Back | Forward | Home | Reload | Images | Open | Print | Find | Stop

Grade Level   K–6

Activity Title   Kids-Weathernet

Description   Kids-Weathernet is a weekly exchange of weather data among schools around the world.

Internet Address   E-mail: echo@triton.unm.edu

Teaching Tip   Ask students to keep a chart of the weather at their school for one week. Older students can collect weather statistics from local newspapers or other sources. Students can e-mail their weather reports to the address above to share with students throughout the world.

Back | Forward | Home | Reload | Images | Open | Print | Find | Stop

Grade Level   4–6

Activity Title   Mousetrap Powered Vehicle Challenge!

Description   This competition would be a great extension to a lesson on simple machines, complex machines, power, or force. The goal is to design a mousetrap-powered vehicle to go the greatest distance in class.

Internet Address   http://sun.bucknell.edu/~boulter/crayon/

Teaching Tip   Teachers, parents, and students can all be involved in this fun activity. If you choose to participate, you must contact the site for design parameters and racing instructions. In 1994–95, the winner sent his vehicle 79 feet 2 inches (2,413 cm)!

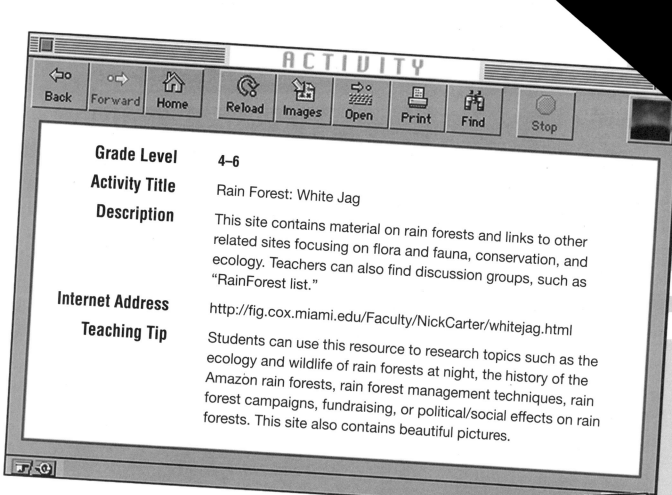

Grade Level 4–6

Activity Title Rain Forest: White Jag

Description This site contains material on rain forests and links to other related sites focusing on flora and fauna, conservation, and ecology. Teachers can also find discussion groups, such as "RainForest list."

Internet Address http://fig.cox.miami.edu/Faculty/NickCarter/whitejag.html

Teaching Tip Students can use this resource to research topics such as the ecology and wildlife of rain forests at night, the history of the Amazon rain forests, rain forest management techniques, rain forest campaigns, fundraising, or political/social effects on rain forests. This site also contains beautiful pictures.

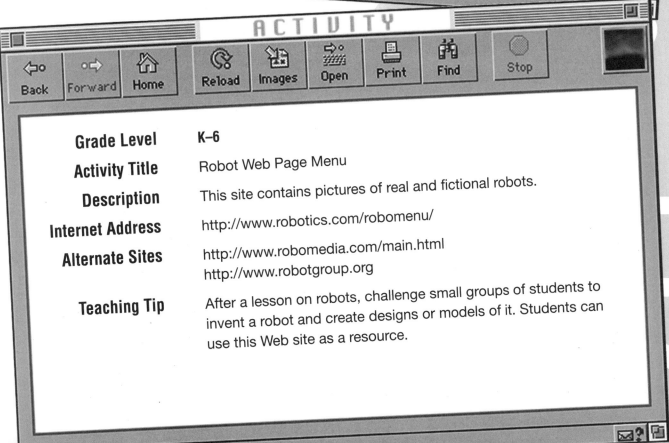

Grade Level K–6

Activity Title Robot Web Page Menu

Description This site contains pictures of real and fictional robots.

Internet Address http://www.robotics.com/robomenu/

Alternate Sites http://www.robomedia.com/main.html
http://www.robotgroup.org

Teaching Tip After a lesson on robots, challenge small groups of students to invent a robot and create designs or models of it. Students can use this Web site as a resource.

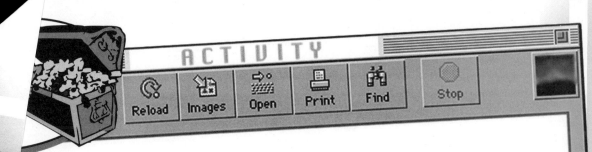

Reload | Images | Open | Print | Find | Stop

Grade Level	**K–6**
Activity Title	Science Gateway
Description	This site provides numerous hyperlinks to scientific areas such as satellite views of earth, aquatic life, bats, frogs, volcanoes, and rain forests. Other links connect to anthropology resources.
Internet Address	http://www.tc.cornell/edu/Edu/MathSciGateway
Teaching Tip	This site can lead teachers and students to many additional science resources. If resources in this chapter do not offer the science activities you are seeking, explore the Internet address above.

Back | Forward | Home | Reload | Images | Open | Print | Find | Stop

Grade Level	**K–6**
Activity Title	View of the Solar System
Description	This site contains links to planet statistics, images, animation, and a glossary. You can download NASA space software to view stars and planets.
Internet Address	http://128.165.1.1/solarsys/
Alternate Sites	http://www.hq.nasa.gov/office/solar_system/ http://www-ssv.jpl.nasa.gov/SSV/SSV_home.html
Teaching Tip	If possible, take students to a planetarium. Then help them download software to view stars and planets on their computers. Students can compare the planetarium show with the simulation. Ask students to make predictions about the monthly movements of the Big Dipper or Orion, then view the constellations in the night sky.

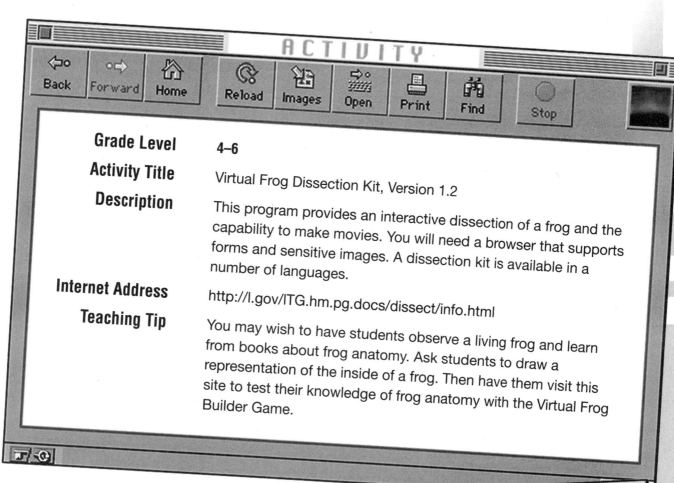

ACTIVITY

Back | Forward | Home | Reload | Images | Open | Print | Find | Stop

Grade Level 4–6

Activity Title Virtual Frog Dissection Kit, Version 1.2

Description This program provides an interactive dissection of a frog and the capability to make movies. You will need a browser that supports forms and sensitive images. A dissection kit is available in a number of languages.

Internet Address http://l.gov/ITG.hm.pg.docs/dissect/info.html

Teaching Tip You may wish to have students observe a living frog and learn from books about frog anatomy. Ask students to draw a representation of the inside of a frog. Then have them visit this site to test their knowledge of frog anatomy with the Virtual Frog Builder Game.

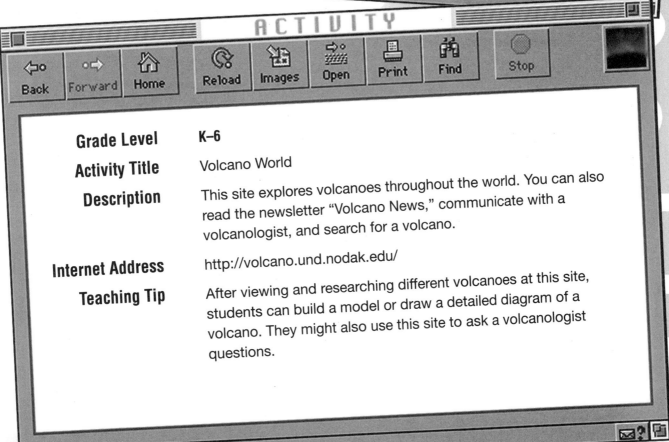

ACTIVITY

Back | Forward | Home | Reload | Images | Open | Print | Find | Stop

Grade Level K–6

Activity Title Volcano World

Description This site explores volcanoes throughout the world. You can also read the newsletter "Volcano News," communicate with a volcanologist, and search for a volcano.

Internet Address http://volcano.und.nodak.edu/

Teaching Tip After viewing and researching different volcanoes at this site, students can build a model or draw a detailed diagram of a volcano. They might also use this site to ask a volcanologist questions.

Grade Level	4–6
Activity Title	Weather Underground: A Complete U.S. Weather Service
Description	This site provides weather forecasts for U.S. regions and cities.
Internet Address	Telnet: madlab.sprl.umich.edu 3000
Teaching Tip	Use this activity to extend a unit on weather and climate. Ask students to look at the current weather for the following cities: Orlando, Detroit, Seattle, and Phoenix. Ask students to predict the weather in each city in one week. They can use this site to track the weather each day and check how their predictions matched the actual weather.

Grade Level	K–6
Activity Title	A Whale of a Tale: Whales
Description	This site includes teacher resources, student activities, projects, and other topics related to whales.
Internet Address	http://curry.edschool.Virginia.EDU:80/~kpj 5e/Whales/
Teaching Tip	This site is a helpful reference for students who are researching whales. Guide students to the activities and topics within this site that would help them with their projects. Have small groups of students choose a project at the site to complete.

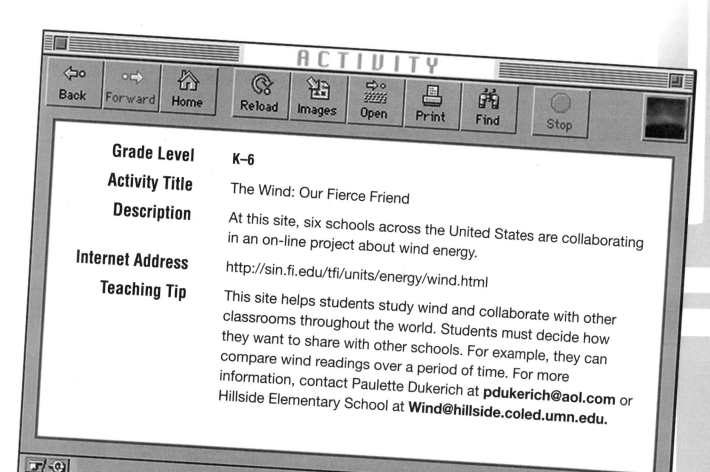

Back | Forward | Home | Reload | Images | Open | Print | Find | Stop

Grade Level K–6

Activity Title The Wind: Our Fierce Friend

Description At this site, six schools across the United States are collaborating in an on-line project about wind energy.

Internet Address http://sin.fi.edu/tfi/units/energy/wind.html

Teaching Tip This site helps students study wind and collaborate with other classrooms throughout the world. Students must decide how they want to share with other schools. For example, they can compare wind readings over a period of time. For more information, contact Paulette Dukerich at **pdukerich@aol.com** or Hillside Elementary School at **Wind@hillside.coled.umn.edu.**

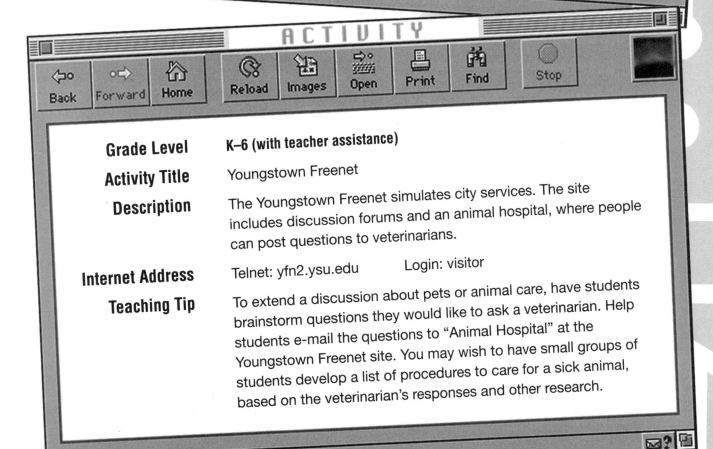

Back | Forward | Home | Reload | Images | Open | Print | Find | Stop

Grade Level K–6 (with teacher assistance)

Activity Title Youngstown Freenet

Description The Youngstown Freenet simulates city services. The site includes discussion forums and an animal hospital, where people can post questions to veterinarians.

Internet Address Telnet: yfn2.ysu.edu   Login: visitor

Teaching Tip To extend a discussion about pets or animal care, have students brainstorm questions they would like to ask a veterinarian. Help students e-mail the questions to "Animal Hospital" at the Youngstown Freenet site. You may wish to have small groups of students develop a list of procedures to care for a sick animal, based on the veterinarian's responses and other research.

Chapter 10
Social Studies

In this chapter you will find a number of the most beneficial and enjoyable social studies resources for K–6 teachers. This area includes regions and peoples, current events, government, geography, and history.

Social Studies Resources	K	1	2	3	4	5	6
1492 Columbus			*	*	*	*	*
Camelot					*	*	*
Favorite Fashions Around the World					*	*	*
Flags: Symbols Through History	*	*	*	*	*	*	*
The Freedom Shrine						*	*
The French American School	*	*	*	*	*	*	*
Guide to New York City					*	*	*
History/Social Studies Resources					*	*	*
Intercultural E-Mail Classroom Connections	*	*	*	*		*	*
Memories Mail List					*	*	*
Mr. Dahncke's Intermediate Multiage Classroom's Home Page					*	*	
Native Web: First Nation Peoples	*	*	*	*	*	*	*
Newsday					*	*	*
NEWSLINK	*	*	*	*	*	*	*
Orienteering					*	*	*
This Day in History					*	*	*
USA Citylink Project	*	*	*	*	*	*	*
Welcome to the "Old Rock School"!	*	*	*	*	*	*	*
The White House	*	*	*	*	*	*	*
World's Youth News	*	*	*	*	*	*	*
	K	1	2	3	4	5	6

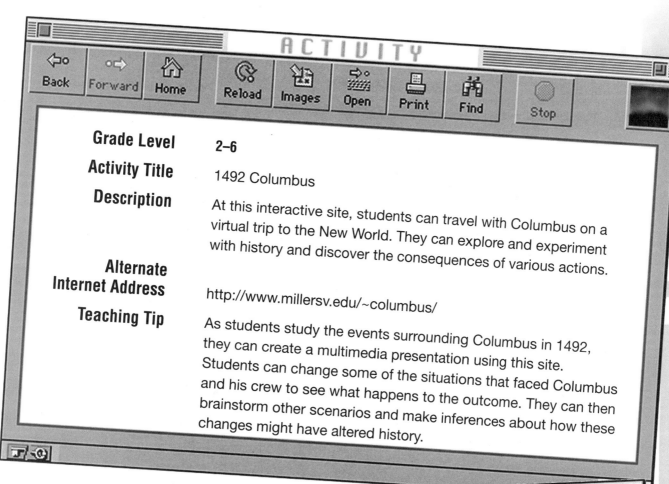

ACTIVITY

Back Forward Home Reload Images Open Print Find Stop

Grade Level 2–6

Activity Title 1492 Columbus

Description At this interactive site, students can travel with Columbus on a virtual trip to the New World. They can explore and experiment with history and discover the consequences of various actions.

Alternate Internet Address http://www.millersv.edu/~columbus/

Teaching Tip As students study the events surrounding Columbus in 1492, they can create a multimedia presentation using this site. Students can change some of the situations that faced Columbus and his crew to see what happens to the outcome. They can then brainstorm other scenarios and make inferences about how these changes might have altered history.

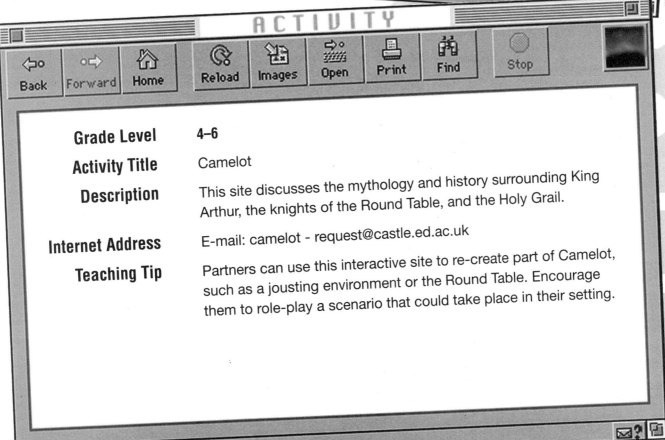

ACTIVITY

Back Forward Home Reload Images Open Print Find Stop

Grade Level 4–6

Activity Title Camelot

Description This site discusses the mythology and history surrounding King Arthur, the knights of the Round Table, and the Holy Grail.

Internet Address E-mail: camelot - request@castle.ed.ac.uk

Teaching Tip Partners can use this interactive site to re-create part of Camelot, such as a jousting environment or the Round Table. Encourage them to role-play a scenario that could take place in their setting.

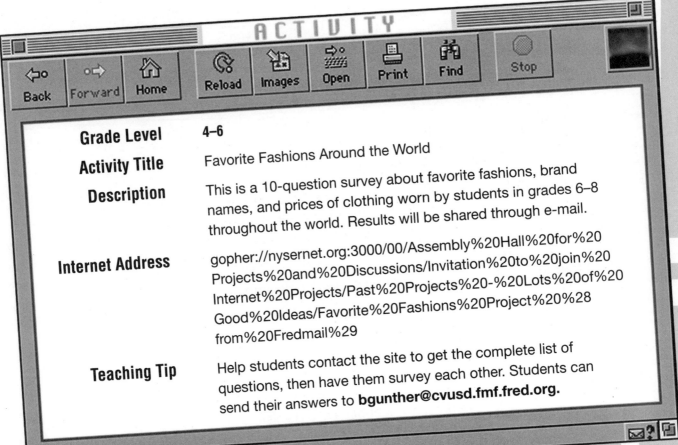

Back | Forward | Home | Reload | Images | Open | Print | Find | Stop

Grade Level	4–6
Activity Title	Favorite Fashions Around the World
Description	This is a 10-question survey about favorite fashions, brand names, and prices of clothing worn by students in grades 6–8 throughout the world. Results will be shared through e-mail.
Internet Address	gopher://nysernet.org:3000/00/Assembly%20Hall%20for%20 Projects%20and%20Discussions/Invitation%20to%20join%20 Internet%20Projects/Past%20Projects%20-%20Lots%20of%20 Good%20Ideas/Favorite%20Fashions%20Project%20%28 from%20Fredmail%29
Teaching Tip	Help students contact the site to get the complete list of questions, then have them survey each other. Students can send their answers to **bgunther@cvusd.fmf.fred.org**.

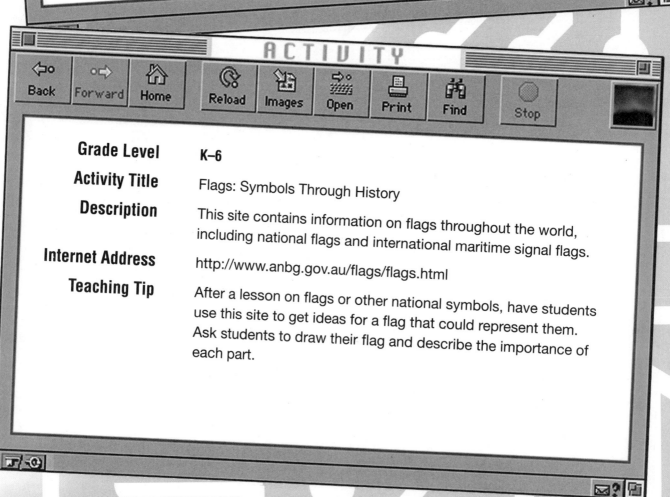

Back | Forward | Home | Reload | Images | Open | Print | Find | Stop

Grade Level	K–6
Activity Title	Flags: Symbols Through History
Description	This site contains information on flags throughout the world, including national flags and international maritime signal flags.
Internet Address	http://www.anbg.gov.au/flags/flags.html
Teaching Tip	After a lesson on flags or other national symbols, have students use this site to get ideas for a flag that could represent them. Ask students to draw their flag and describe the importance of each part.

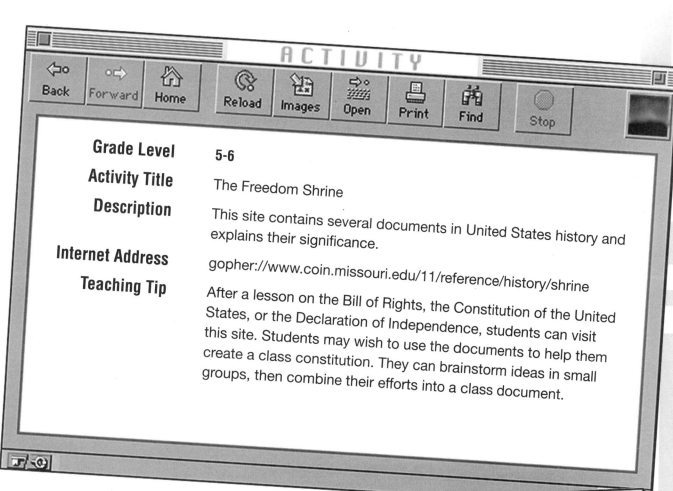

Grade Level 5-6

Activity Title The Freedom Shrine

Description This site contains several documents in United States history and explains their significance.

Internet Address gopher://www.coin.missouri.edu/11/reference/history/shrine

Teaching Tip After a lesson on the Bill of Rights, the Constitution of the United States, or the Declaration of Independence, students can visit this site. Students may wish to use the documents to help them create a class constitution. They can brainstorm ideas in small groups, then combine their efforts into a class document.

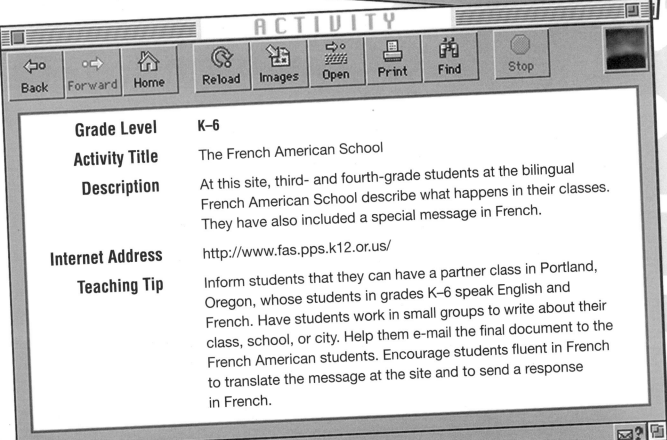

Grade Level K–6

Activity Title The French American School

Description At this site, third- and fourth-grade students at the bilingual French American School describe what happens in their classes. They have also included a special message in French.

Internet Address http://www.fas.pps.k12.or.us/

Teaching Tip Inform students that they can have a partner class in Portland, Oregon, whose students in grades K–6 speak English and French. Have students work in small groups to write about their class, school, or city. Help them e-mail the final document to the French American students. Encourage students fluent in French to translate the message at the site and to send a response in French.

Grade Level	4–6
Activity Title	Guide to New York City
Description	This site contains information about New York City, including government addresses, services for kids and families, services for consumer complaints, and information on parks and recreation.
Internet Address	http://www.pubadvocate.nyc.gov/~advocate/greenbook/greenbook.html
Teaching Tip	After a lesson on urban communities, invite students to list things they want to learn about New York City. A few examples would be *What is the address and phone number for Yankee Stadium? Where would you go to get a dog license?* Then ask students to use this site to find answers.

Treasure Chest Site!

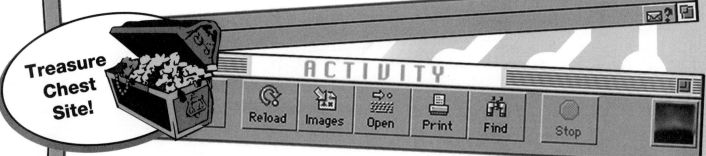

Grade Level	4–6
Activity Title	History/Social Studies Resources
Description	This is a great site to connect with many other areas of the Internet, including "The Ancient World," "Flags," "Maps," "Government," and "History."
Internet Address	http://www.acm.cps.msu.edu/~spiveyed/History.html
Teaching Tip	Ask students to find "History and Historiography." Have them work in small groups to make a chart of the topics. If they are not sure about a term, they can click on the topic and read about it. Have groups explain their charts to other groups.

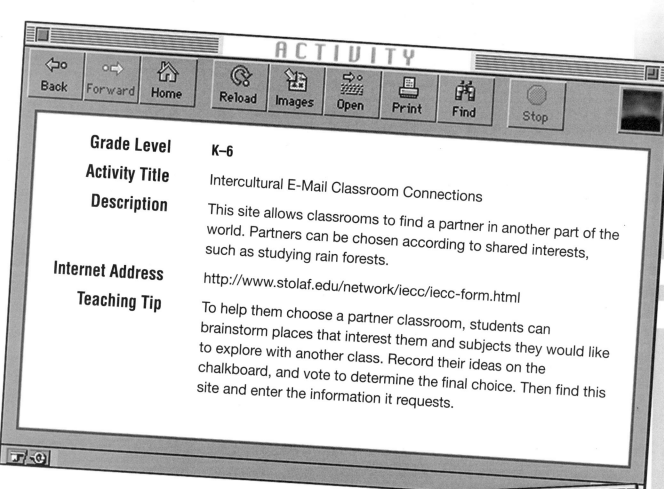

ACTIVITY

Back | Forward | Home | Reload | Images | Open | Print | Find | Stop

Grade Level	K–6
Activity Title	Intercultural E-Mail Classroom Connections
Description	This site allows classrooms to find a partner in another part of the world. Partners can be chosen according to shared interests, such as studying rain forests.
Internet Address	http://www.stolaf.edu/network/iecc/iecc-form.html
Teaching Tip	To help them choose a partner classroom, students can brainstorm places that interest them and subjects they would like to explore with another class. Record their ideas on the chalkboard, and vote to determine the final choice. Then find this site and enter the information it requests.

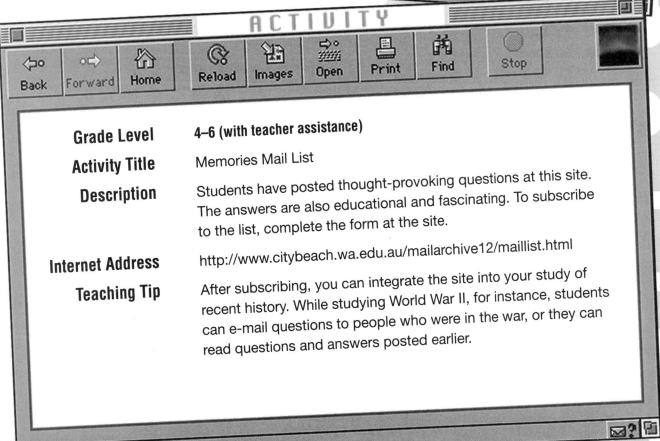

ACTIVITY

Back | Forward | Home | Reload | Images | Open | Print | Find | Stop

Grade Level	4–6 (with teacher assistance)
Activity Title	Memories Mail List
Description	Students have posted thought-provoking questions at this site. The answers are also educational and fascinating. To subscribe to the list, complete the form at the site.
Internet Address	http://www.citybeach.wa.edu.au/mailarchive12/maillist.html
Teaching Tip	After subscribing, you can integrate the site into your study of recent history. While studying World War II, for instance, students can e-mail questions to people who were in the war, or they can read questions and answers posted earlier.

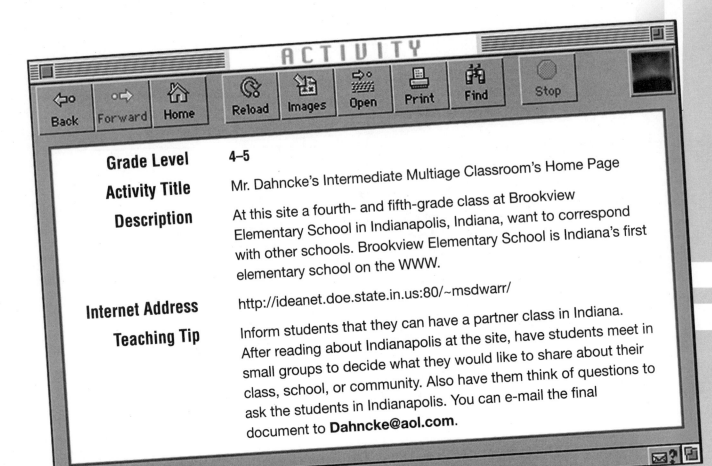

Back Forward Home Reload Images Open Print Find Stop

Grade Level 4–5

Activity Title Mr. Dahncke's Intermediate Multiage Classroom's Home Page

Description At this site a fourth- and fifth-grade class at Brookview Elementary School in Indianapolis, Indiana, want to correspond with other schools. Brookview Elementary School is Indiana's first elementary school on the WWW.

Internet Address http://ideanet.doe.state.in.us:80/~msdwarr/

Teaching Tip Inform students that they can have a partner class in Indiana. After reading about Indianapolis at the site, have students meet in small groups to decide what they would like to share about their class, school, or community. Also have them think of questions to ask the students in Indianapolis. You can e-mail the final document to **Dahncke@aol.com**.

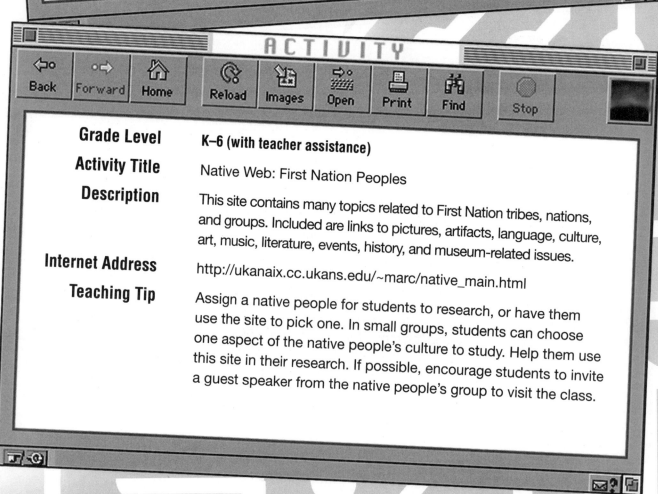

Back Forward Home Reload Images Open Print Find Stop

Grade Level K–6 (with teacher assistance)

Activity Title Native Web: First Nation Peoples

Description This site contains many topics related to First Nation tribes, nations, and groups. Included are links to pictures, artifacts, language, culture, art, music, literature, events, history, and museum-related issues.

Internet Address http://ukanaix.cc.ukans.edu/~marc/native_main.html

Teaching Tip Assign a native people for students to research, or have them use the site to pick one. In small groups, students can choose one aspect of the native people's culture to study. Help them use this site in their research. If possible, encourage students to invite a guest speaker from the native people's group to visit the class.

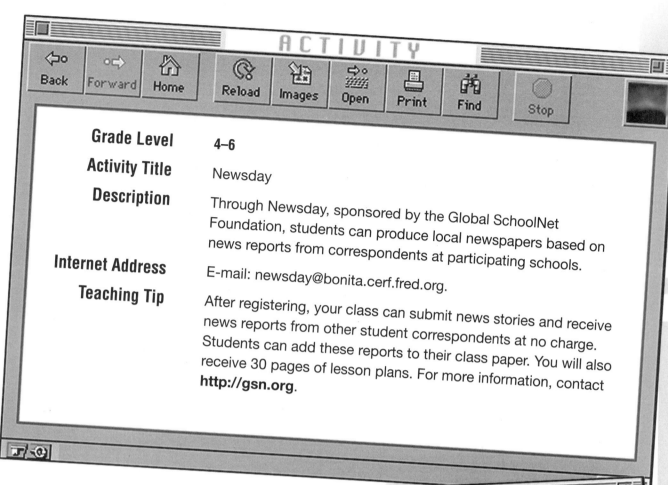

Back　Forward　Home　Reload　Images　Open　Print　Find　Stop

Grade Level	**4–6**
Activity Title	Newsday
Description	Through Newsday, sponsored by the Global SchoolNet Foundation, students can produce local newspapers based on news reports from correspondents at participating schools.
Internet Address	E-mail: newsday@bonita.cerf.fred.org.
Teaching Tip	After registering, your class can submit news stories and receive news reports from other student correspondents at no charge. Students can add these reports to their class paper. You will also receive 30 pages of lesson plans. For more information, contact **http://gsn.org**.

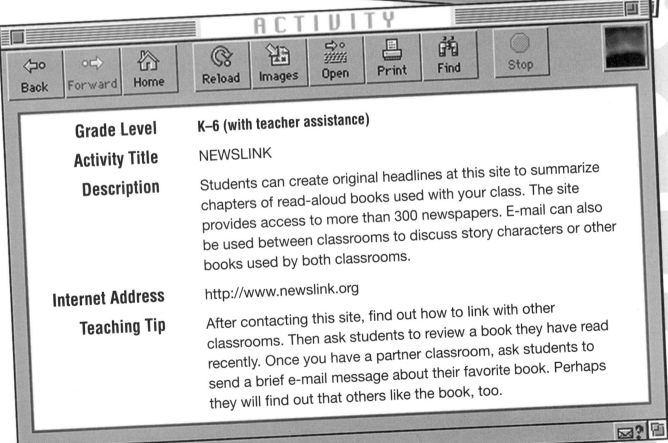

Back　Forward　Home　Reload　Images　Open　Print　Find　Stop

Grade Level	**K–6 (with teacher assistance)**
Activity Title	NEWSLINK
Description	Students can create original headlines at this site to summarize chapters of read-aloud books used with your class. The site provides access to more than 300 newspapers. E-mail can also be used between classrooms to discuss story characters or other books used by both classrooms.
Internet Address	http://www.newslink.org
Teaching Tip	After contacting this site, find out how to link with other classrooms. Then ask students to review a book they have read recently. Once you have a partner classroom, ask students to send a brief e-mail message about their favorite book. Perhaps they will find out that others like the book, too.

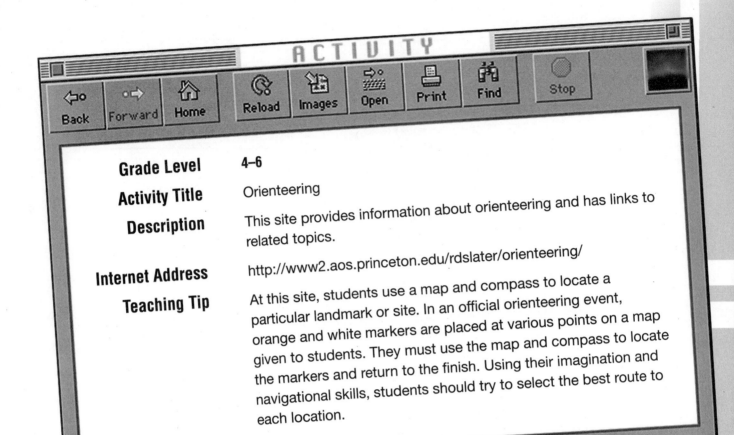

Grade Level	4–6
Activity Title	Orienteering
Description	This site provides information about orienteering and has links to related topics.
Internet Address	http://www2.aos.princeton.edu/rdslater/orienteering/
Teaching Tip	At this site, students use a map and compass to locate a particular landmark or site. In an official orienteering event, orange and white markers are placed at various points on a map given to students. They must use the map and compass to locate the markers and return to the finish. Using their imagination and navigational skills, students should try to select the best route to each location.

ACTIVITY

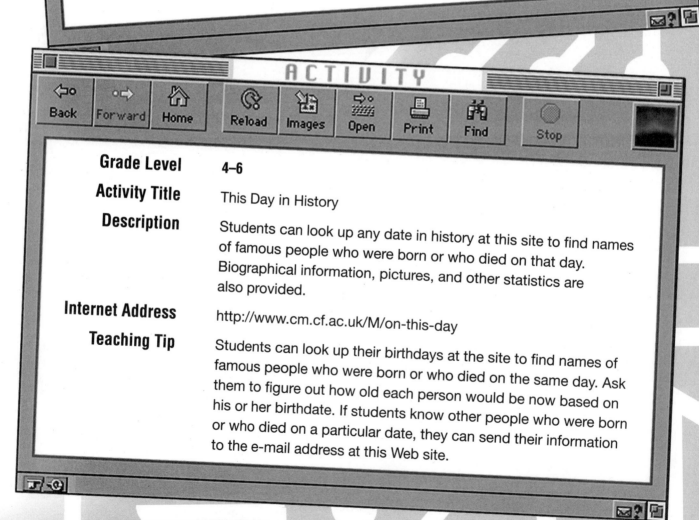

Grade Level	4–6
Activity Title	This Day in History
Description	Students can look up any date in history at this site to find names of famous people who were born or who died on that day. Biographical information, pictures, and other statistics are also provided.
Internet Address	http://www.cm.cf.ac.uk/M/on-this-day
Teaching Tip	Students can look up their birthdays at the site to find names of famous people who were born or who died on the same day. Ask them to figure out how old each person would be now based on his or her birthdate. If students know other people who were born or who died on a particular date, they can send their information to the e-mail address at this Web site.

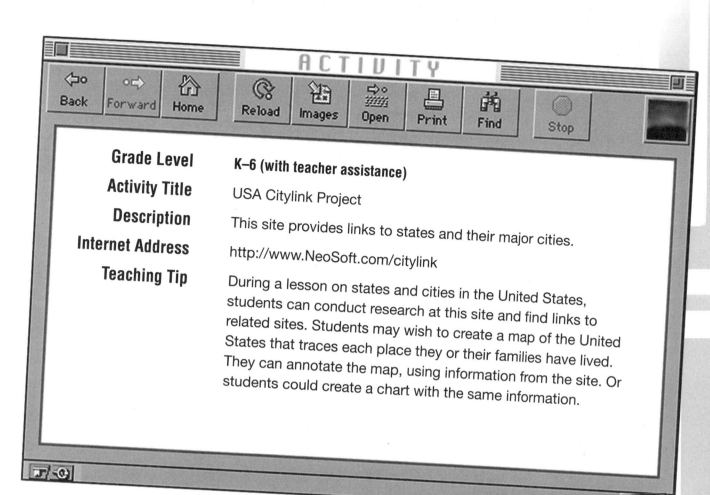

Back   Forward   Home   Reload   Images   Open   Print   Find   Stop

Grade Level	**K–6 (with teacher assistance)**
Activity Title	USA Citylink Project
Description	This site provides links to states and their major cities.
Internet Address	http://www.NeoSoft.com/citylink
Teaching Tip	During a lesson on states and cities in the United States, students can conduct research at this site and find links to related sites. Students may wish to create a map of the United States that traces each place they or their families have lived. They can annotate the map, using information from the site. Or students could create a chart with the same information.

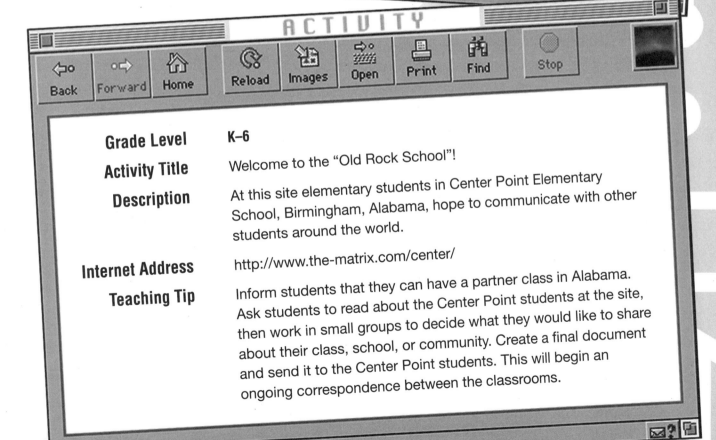

Back   Forward   Home   Reload   Images   Open   Print   Find   Stop

Grade Level	**K–6**
Activity Title	Welcome to the "Old Rock School"!
Description	At this site elementary students in Center Point Elementary School, Birmingham, Alabama, hope to communicate with other students around the world.
Internet Address	http://www.the-matrix.com/center/
Teaching Tip	Inform students that they can have a partner class in Alabama. Ask students to read about the Center Point students at the site, then work in small groups to decide what they would like to share about their class, school, or community. Create a final document and send it to the Center Point students. This will begin an ongoing correspondence between the classrooms.

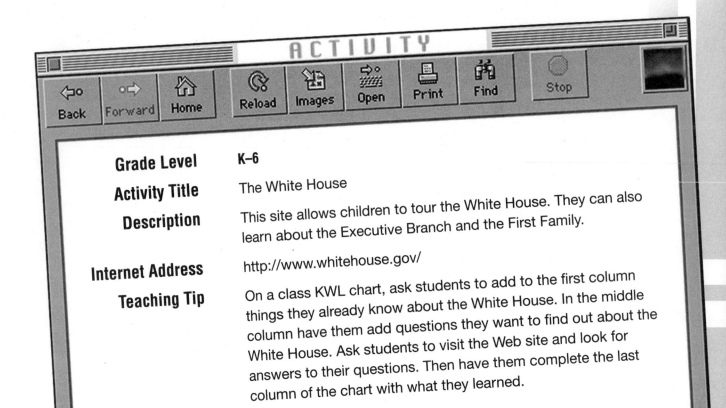

Grade Level K–6

Activity Title The White House

Description This site allows children to tour the White House. They can also learn about the Executive Branch and the First Family.

Internet Address http://www.whitehouse.gov/

Teaching Tip On a class KWL chart, ask students to add to the first column things they already know about the White House. In the middle column have them add questions they want to find out about the White House. Ask students to visit the Web site and look for answers to their questions. Then have them complete the last column of the chart with what they learned.

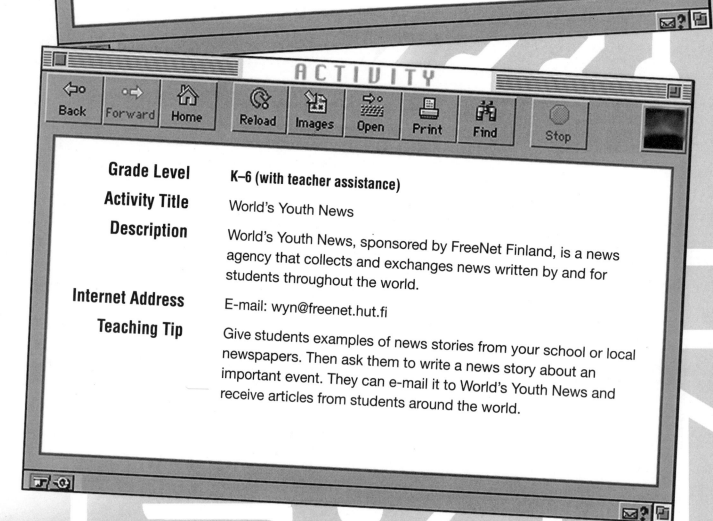

Grade Level K–6 (with teacher assistance)

Activity Title World's Youth News

Description World's Youth News, sponsored by FreeNet Finland, is a news agency that collects and exchanges news written by and for students throughout the world.

Internet Address E-mail: wyn@freenet.hut.fi

Teaching Tip Give students examples of news stories from your school or local newspapers. Then ask them to write a news story about an important event. They can e-mail it to World's Youth News and receive articles from students around the world.

Chapter 11
Health, Nutrition, and Physical Fitness

In this chapter you will find a number of the most beneficial and enjoyable resources for K–6 teachers to use in the areas of health, nutrition, and physical fitness.

Health, Nutrition, and Physical Fitness Resources	K	1	2	3	4	5	6
Alcohol and Drug Abuse Education for Elementary Children	*	*	*	*	*	*	*
The Fitness Challenge	*	*	*	*	*	*	*
Food Guide Pyramid	*	*	*	*	*	*	*
Food in Malawi	*	*	*	*	*	*	*
Fruit and Nutrition Center					*	*	*
Fun Stuff: Fun with Fruits and Vegetables Kids Cookbook					*	*	*
Health Ed List					*	*	*
Health Resources				*	*	*	*
Healthy Herb	*	*	*	*			
The Heart	*	*	*	*	*	*	*
Home Page for Soccer!	*	*	*	*	*	*	*
International Games					*	*	*
Let the Light Shine In: A Look at the Iris	*	*	*	*			
The Longevity Game	*	*	*	*	*	*	*
Minerals			*	*	*	*	*
Presidential Fitness Program	*	*	*	*	*	*	*
Sports Video Clips	*	*	*	*	*	*	*
Ten Tips for Healthy Eating and Physical Activity for You					*	*	*
Vitamins			*	*	*	*	*
Volleyball					*	*	*
	K	1	2	3	4	5	6

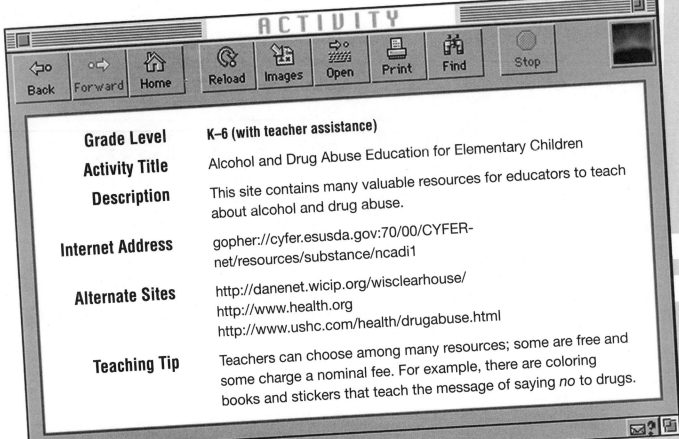

Back Forward Home Reload Images Open Print Find Stop

Grade Level K–6 (with teacher assistance)

Activity Title Alcohol and Drug Abuse Education for Elementary Children

Description This site contains many valuable resources for educators to teach about alcohol and drug abuse.

Internet Address gopher://cyfer.esusda.gov:70/00/CYFER-net/resources/substance/ncadi1

Alternate Sites http://danenet.wicip.org/wisclearhouse/
http://www.health.org
http://www.ushc.com/health/drugabuse.html

Teaching Tip Teachers can choose among many resources; some are free and some charge a nominal fee. For example, there are coloring books and stickers that teach the message of saying *no* to drugs.

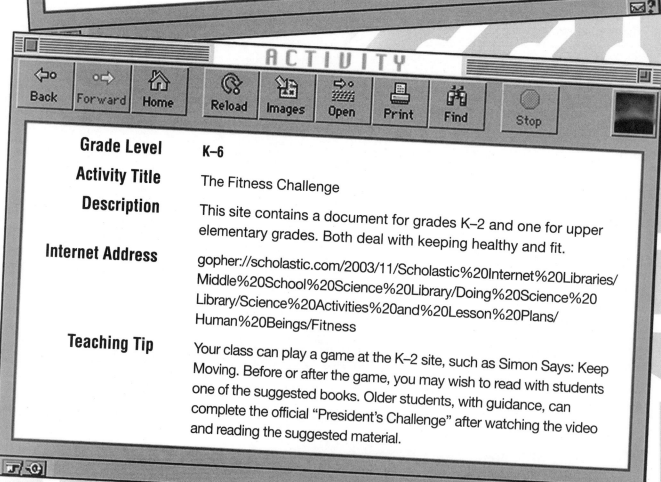

Back Forward Home Reload Images Open Print Find Stop

Grade Level K–6

Activity Title The Fitness Challenge

Description This site contains a document for grades K–2 and one for upper elementary grades. Both deal with keeping healthy and fit.

Internet Address gopher://scholastic.com/2003/11/Scholastic%20Internet%20Libraries/Middle%20School%20Science%20Library/Doing%20Science%20Library/Science%20Activities%20and%20Lesson%20Plans/Human%20Beings/Fitness

Teaching Tip Your class can play a game at the K–2 site, such as Simon Says: Keep Moving. Before or after the game, you may wish to read with students one of the suggested books. Older students, with guidance, can complete the official "President's Challenge" after watching the video and reading the suggested material.

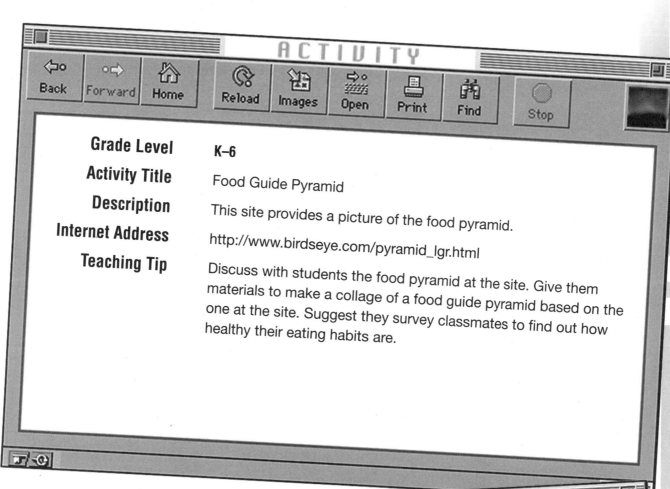

ACTIVITY

Back Forward Home Reload Images Open Print Find Stop

Grade Level	K–6
Activity Title	Food Guide Pyramid
Description	This site provides a picture of the food pyramid.
Internet Address	http://www.birdseye.com/pyramid_lgr.html
Teaching Tip	Discuss with students the food pyramid at the site. Give them materials to make a collage of a food guide pyramid based on the one at the site. Suggest they survey classmates to find out how healthy their eating habits are.

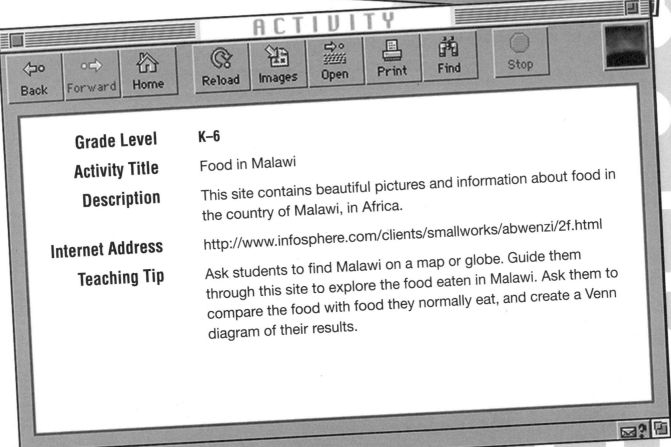

ACTIVITY

Back Forward Home Reload Images Open Print Find Stop

Grade Level	K–6
Activity Title	Food in Malawi
Description	This site contains beautiful pictures and information about food in the country of Malawi, in Africa.
Internet Address	http://www.infosphere.com/clients/smallworks/abwenzi/2f.html
Teaching Tip	Ask students to find Malawi on a map or globe. Guide them through this site to explore the food eaten in Malawi. Ask them to compare the food with food they normally eat, and create a Venn diagram of their results.

Health, Nutrition, and Physical Fitness

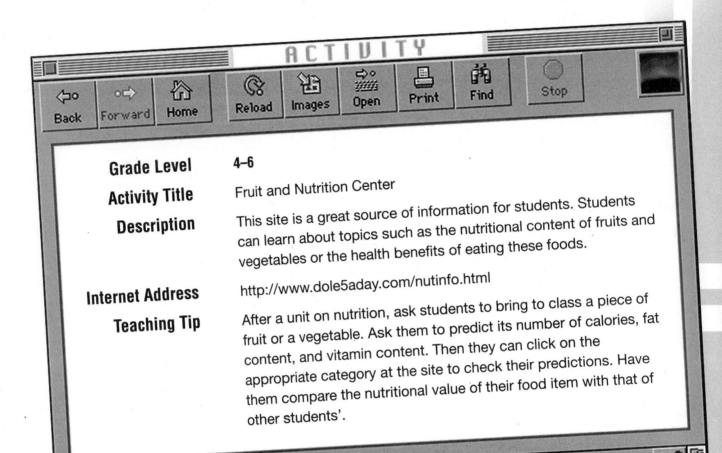

Grade Level   4–6

Activity Title   Fruit and Nutrition Center

Description   This site is a great source of information for students. Students can learn about topics such as the nutritional content of fruits and vegetables or the health benefits of eating these foods.

Internet Address   http://www.dole5aday.com/nutinfo.html

Teaching Tip   After a unit on nutrition, ask students to bring to class a piece of fruit or a vegetable. Ask them to predict its number of calories, fat content, and vitamin content. Then they can click on the appropriate category at the site to check their predictions. Have them compare the nutritional value of their food item with that of other students'.

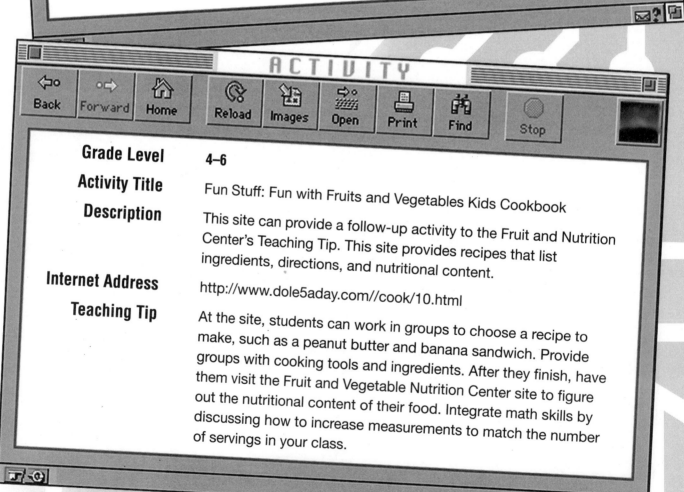

Grade Level   4–6

Activity Title   Fun Stuff: Fun with Fruits and Vegetables Kids Cookbook

Description   This site can provide a follow-up activity to the Fruit and Nutrition Center's Teaching Tip. This site provides recipes that list ingredients, directions, and nutritional content.

Internet Address   http://www.dole5aday.com//cook/10.html

Teaching Tip   At the site, students can work in groups to choose a recipe to make, such as a peanut butter and banana sandwich. Provide groups with cooking tools and ingredients. After they finish, have them visit the Fruit and Vegetable Nutrition Center site to figure out the nutritional content of their food. Integrate math skills by discussing how to increase measurements to match the number of servings in your class.

Grade Level	4–6 (with teacher assistance)
Activity Title	Health Ed List
Description	This is an excellent resource for teachers. It contains links to other sites such as "How Is AIDS Transmitted?" "Stretching and Flexibility," and "The Visible Human Project."
Internet Address	http://www.tc.cornell.edu:80/Edu/MathSciGateway/medicine.html
Teaching Tip	This would be a great resource for older students to use when studying the human body or diseases that can affect it. The pictures should be carefully previewed before allowing students to view them.

Treasure
Chest
Site!

Grade Level	3–6
Activity Title	Health Resources
Description	This site contains many practical and valuable lessons in health, nutrition, and fitness.
Internet Address	gopher://ericir.syr.edu:70/77/Lesson/.lesson/lessons?health
Teaching Tip	This site could be used in many ways, for example: click on "Health: What Causes Tooth Decay?" This lesson uses vinegar and egg shells in a simulation of teeth decomposition to help students understand the causes and implications of tooth decay.

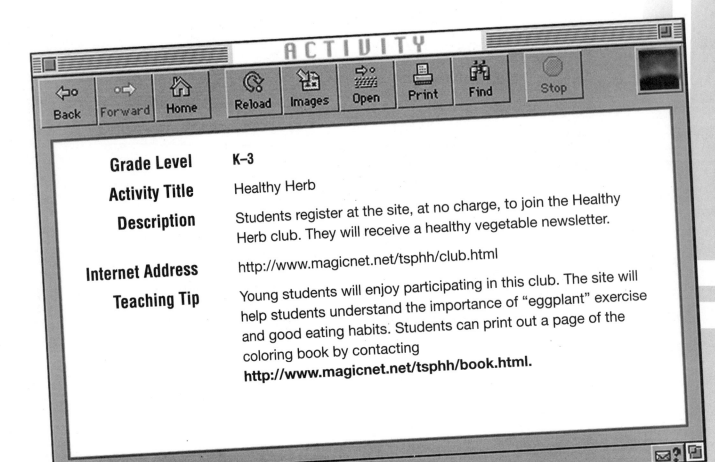

Grade Level   K–3

Activity Title   Healthy Herb

Description   Students register at the site, at no charge, to join the Healthy Herb club. They will receive a healthy vegetable newsletter.

Internet Address   http://www.magicnet.net/tsphh/club.html

Teaching Tip   Young students will enjoy participating in this club. The site will help students understand the importance of "eggplant" exercise and good eating habits. Students can print out a page of the coloring book by contacting **http://www.magicnet.net/tsphh/book.html.**

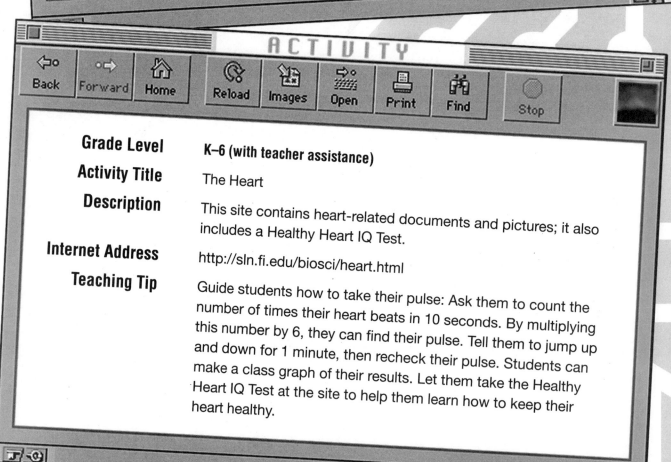

Grade Level   K–6 (with teacher assistance)

Activity Title   The Heart

Description   This site contains heart-related documents and pictures; it also includes a Healthy Heart IQ Test.

Internet Address   http://sln.fi.edu/biosci/heart.html

Teaching Tip   Guide students how to take their pulse: Ask them to count the number of times their heart beats in 10 seconds. By multiplying this number by 6, they can find their pulse. Tell them to jump up and down for 1 minute, then recheck their pulse. Students can make a class graph of their results. Let them take the Healthy Heart IQ Test at the site to help them learn how to keep their heart healthy.

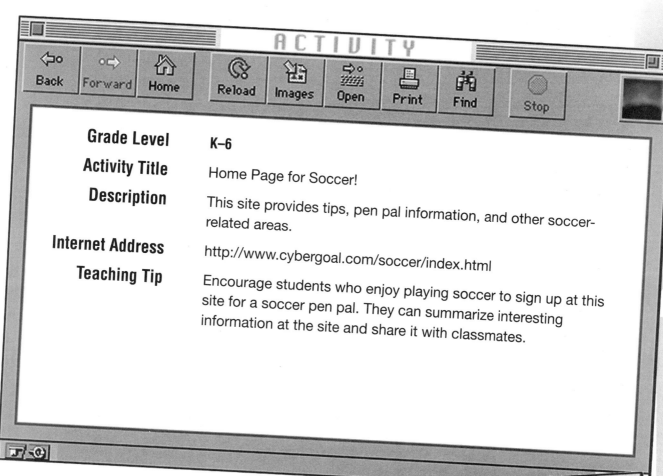

Grade Level	K–6
Activity Title	Home Page for Soccer!
Description	This site provides tips, pen pal information, and other soccer-related areas.
Internet Address	http://www.cybergoal.com/soccer/index.html
Teaching Tip	Encourage students who enjoy playing soccer to sign up at this site for a soccer pen pal. They can summarize interesting information at the site and share it with classmates.

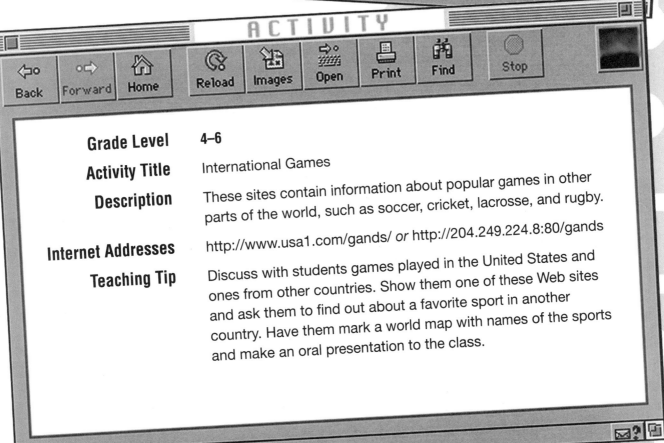

Grade Level	4–6
Activity Title	International Games
Description	These sites contain information about popular games in other parts of the world, such as soccer, cricket, lacrosse, and rugby.
Internet Addresses	http://www.usa1.com/gands/ or http://204.249.224.8:80/gands
Teaching Tip	Discuss with students games played in the United States and ones from other countries. Show them one of these Web sites and ask them to find out about a favorite sport in another country. Have them mark a world map with names of the sports and make an oral presentation to the class.

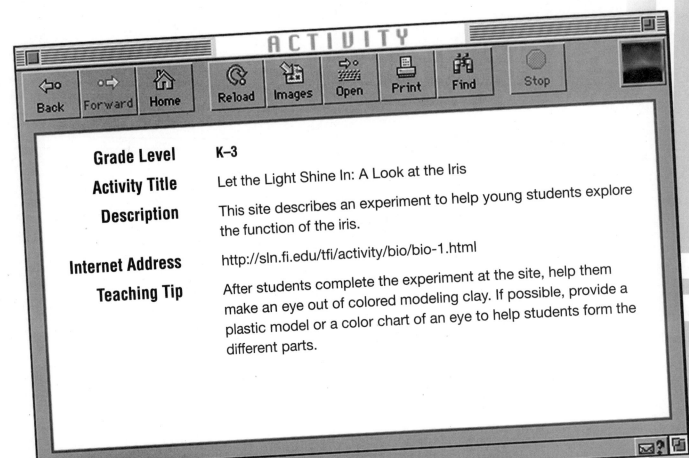

Grade Level	**K–3**
Activity Title	Let the Light Shine In: A Look at the Iris
Description	This site describes an experiment to help young students explore the function of the iris.
Internet Address	http://sln.fi.edu/tfi/activity/bio/bio-1.html
Teaching Tip	After students complete the experiment at the site, help them make an eye out of colored modeling clay. If possible, provide a plastic model or a color chart of an eye to help students form the different parts.

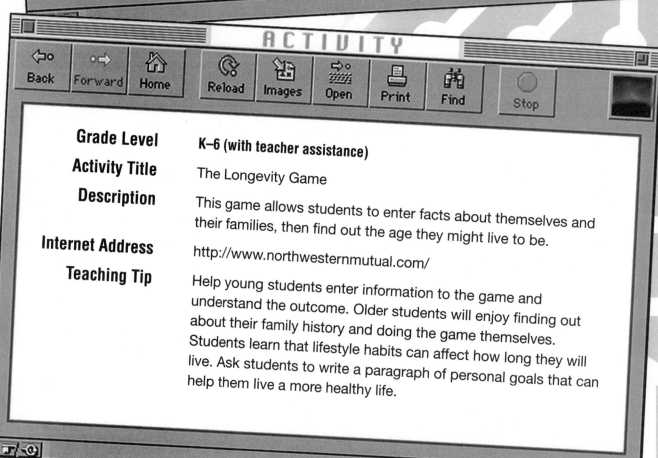

Grade Level	**K–6 (with teacher assistance)**
Activity Title	The Longevity Game
Description	This game allows students to enter facts about themselves and their families, then find out the age they might live to be.
Internet Address	http://www.northwesternmutual.com/
Teaching Tip	Help young students enter information to the game and understand the outcome. Older students will enjoy finding out about their family history and doing the game themselves. Students learn that lifestyle habits can affect how long they will live. Ask students to write a paragraph of personal goals that can help them live a more healthy life.

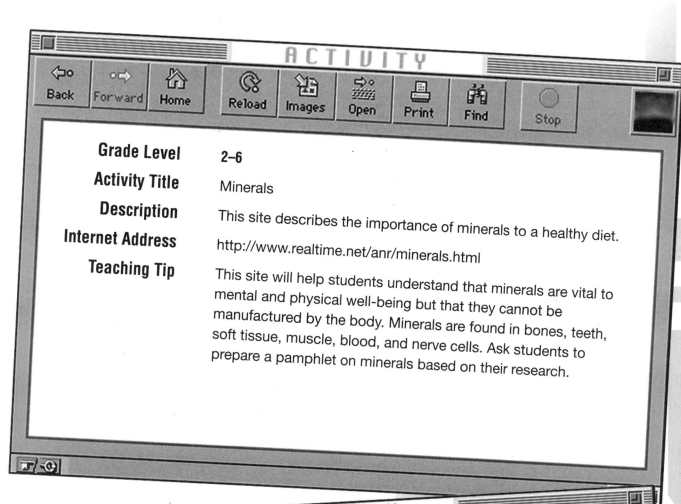

ACTIVITY

Grade Level	2–6
Activity Title	Minerals
Description	This site describes the importance of minerals to a healthy diet.
Internet Address	http://www.realtime.net/anr/minerals.html
Teaching Tip	This site will help students understand that minerals are vital to mental and physical well-being but that they cannot be manufactured by the body. Minerals are found in bones, teeth, soft tissue, muscle, blood, and nerve cells. Ask students to prepare a pamphlet on minerals based on their research.

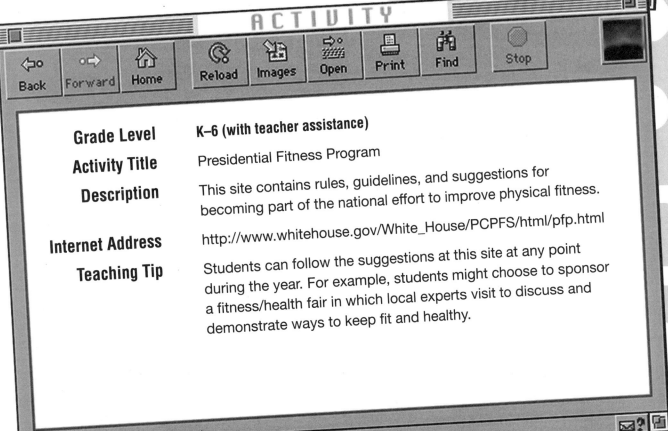

ACTIVITY

Grade Level	K–6 (with teacher assistance)
Activity Title	Presidential Fitness Program
Description	This site contains rules, guidelines, and suggestions for becoming part of the national effort to improve physical fitness.
Internet Address	http://www.whitehouse.gov/White_House/PCPFS/html/pfp.html
Teaching Tip	Students can follow the suggestions at this site at any point during the year. For example, students might choose to sponsor a fitness/health fair in which local experts visit to discuss and demonstrate ways to keep fit and healthy.

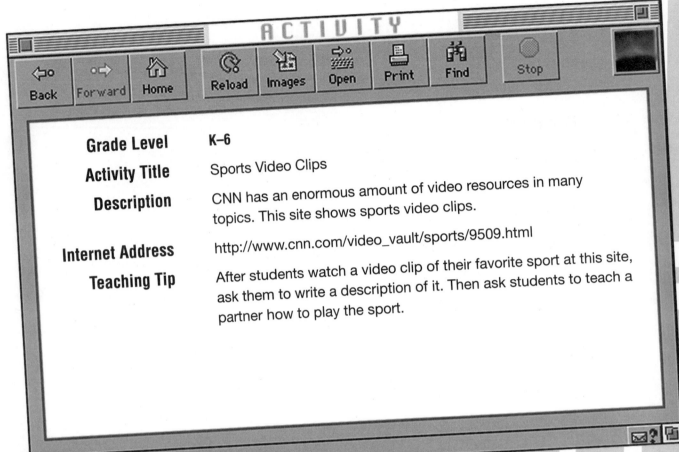

Grade Level	K–6
Activity Title	Sports Video Clips
Description	CNN has an enormous amount of video resources in many topics. This site shows sports video clips.
Internet Address	http://www.cnn.com/video_vault/sports/9509.html
Teaching Tip	After students watch a video clip of their favorite sport at this site, ask them to write a description of it. Then ask students to teach a partner how to play the sport.

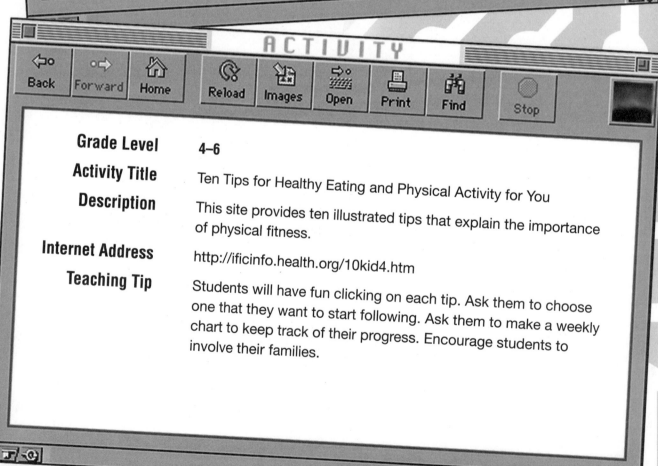

Grade Level	4–6
Activity Title	Ten Tips for Healthy Eating and Physical Activity for You
Description	This site provides ten illustrated tips that explain the importance of physical fitness.
Internet Address	http://ificinfo.health.org/10kid4.htm
Teaching Tip	Students will have fun clicking on each tip. Ask them to choose one that they want to start following. Ask them to make a weekly chart to keep track of their progress. Encourage students to involve their families.

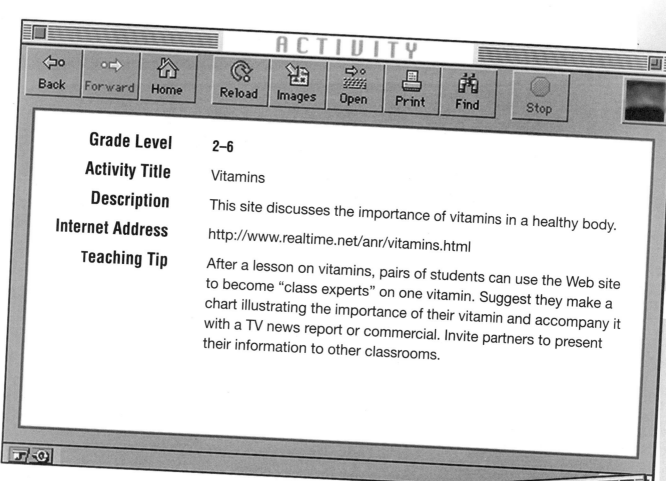

Grade Level 2–6

Activity Title Vitamins

Description This site discusses the importance of vitamins in a healthy body.

Internet Address http://www.realtime.net/anr/vitamins.html

Teaching Tip After a lesson on vitamins, pairs of students can use the Web site to become "class experts" on one vitamin. Suggest they make a chart illustrating the importance of their vitamin and accompany it with a TV news report or commercial. Invite partners to present their information to other classrooms.

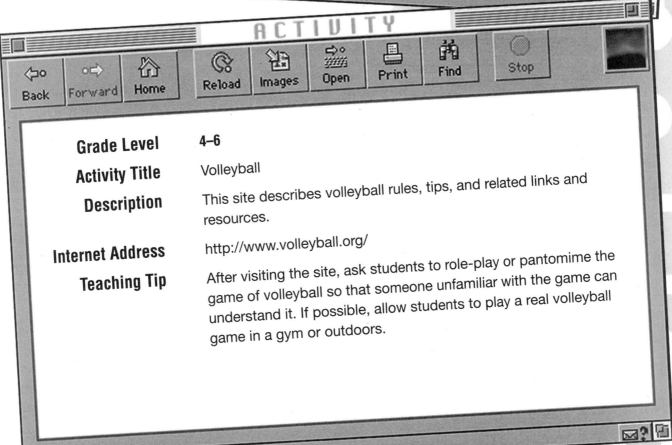

Grade Level 4–6

Activity Title Volleyball

Description This site describes volleyball rules, tips, and related links and resources.

Internet Address http://www.volleyball.org/

Teaching Tip After visiting the site, ask students to role-play or pantomime the game of volleyball so that someone unfamiliar with the game can understand it. If possible, allow students to play a real volleyball game in a gym or outdoors.

Chapter 12

Music, Art, and Dance

This chapter contains a number of the most beneficial and enjoyable resources for K–6 teachers to use in the areas of music, art, and dance.

Music, Art, and Dance Resources	K	1	2	3	4	5	6
Aboriginal Art	*	*	*	*	*	*	*
Abwenzi African Studies	*	*	*	*	*	*	*
Ansel Adams: Photography					*	*	*
Art, Music, and Dance Links	*	*	*	*	*	*	*
Carlos' Coloring Book	*	*	*	*	*	*	*
Crafts for Kids	*	*	*	*	*	*	*
Crayola™	*	*	*	*	*	*	*
Cuban Music	*	*	*	*	*	*	*
Dream Weaver	*	*	*	*	*	*	*
Folk Songs	*	*	*	*	*	*	*
Global Show-n-Tell	*	*	*	*	*	*	*
Himalayas	*	*	*	*	*	*	*
International Writing and Art Contest					*	*	*
Jeconde	*	*	*	*	*	*	*
LEGO™	*	*	*	*	*	*	*
Lite-Brite™	*	*	*	*	*	*	*
Monster Exchange Program					*	*	*
Music Concert	*	*	*	*			
Nowwwhere!			*	*	*	*	*
Origami	*	*	*	*	*	*	*
Sketch the Art Cow	*	*	*	*	*	*	*
	K	1	2	3	4	5	6

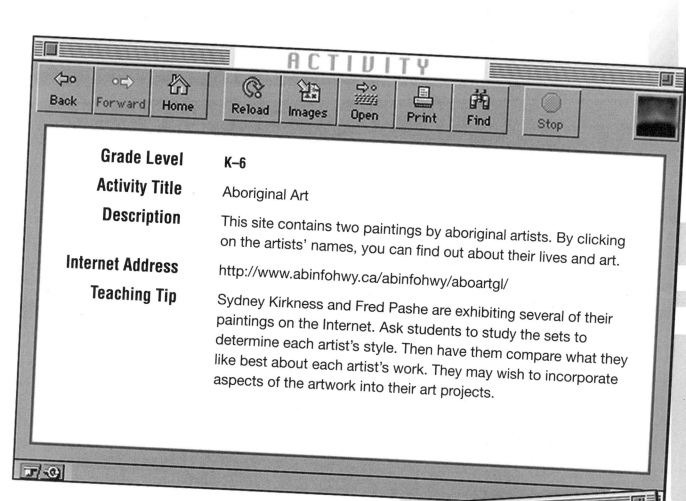

Grade Level	K–6
Activity Title	Aboriginal Art
Description	This site contains two paintings by aboriginal artists. By clicking on the artists' names, you can find out about their lives and art.
Internet Address	http://www.abinfohwy.ca/abinfohwy/aboartgl/
Teaching Tip	Sydney Kirkness and Fred Pashe are exhibiting several of their paintings on the Internet. Ask students to study the sets to determine each artist's style. Then have them compare what they like best about each artist's work. They may wish to incorporate aspects of the artwork into their art projects.

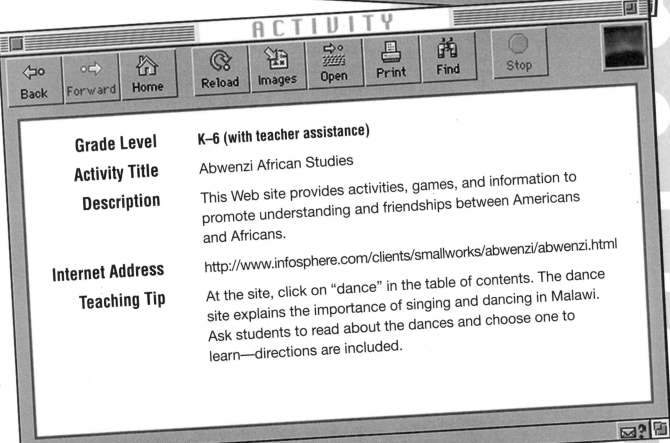

Grade Level	K–6 (with teacher assistance)
Activity Title	Abwenzi African Studies
Description	This Web site provides activities, games, and information to promote understanding and friendships between Americans and Africans.
Internet Address	http://www.infosphere.com/clients/smallworks/abwenzi/abwenzi.html
Teaching Tip	At the site, click on "dance" in the table of contents. The dance site explains the importance of singing and dancing in Malawi. Ask students to read about the dances and choose one to learn—directions are included.

Music, Art, and Dance

Back | Forward | Home | Reload | Images | Open | Print | Find | Stop

Grade Level 4–6

Activity Title Ansel Adams: Photography

Description This site features the photography of Ansel Adams and sound modules in which Adams discusses his works.

Internet Address http://bookweb.cwis.uci.edu:8042/AdamsHome.html

Teaching Tip Some of the writings and essays may be too hard for your students, but they can still benefit from viewing the photographs and listening to Adams. Encourage students to take photographs and put them into a classroom exhibit. Invite students to explain their photos in writing or in person.

Treasure Chest Site!

Reload | Images | Open | Print | Find | Stop

Grade Level K–6 (with teacher assistance)

Activity Title Art, Music, and Dance Links

Description This site contains thousands of links to art, music, and dance sites. Many museums are represented. Preview the sites to make sure the content is grade-level appropriate.

Internet Address http://www.msilink.com/art.html

Teaching Tip This site contains many links to visit throughout the year and to integrate throughout the curriculum. For example, if you are studying Austria, students learn about Austrian folk dancing.

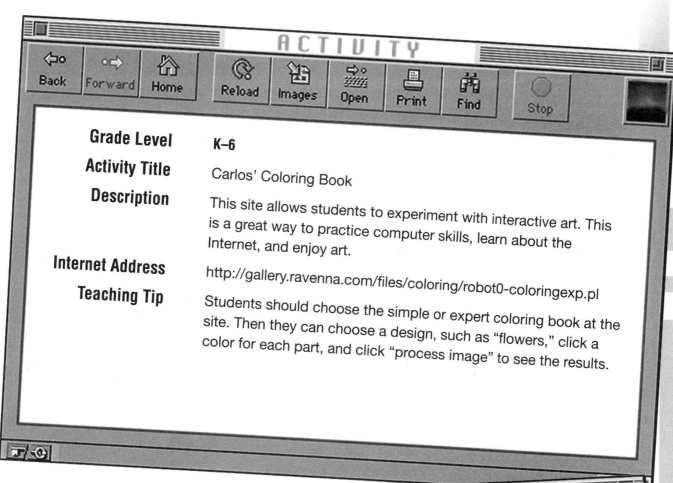

Grade Level	K–6
Activity Title	Carlos' Coloring Book
Description	This site allows students to experiment with interactive art. This is a great way to practice computer skills, learn about the Internet, and enjoy art.
Internet Address	http://gallery.ravenna.com/files/coloring/robot0-coloringexp.pl
Teaching Tip	Students should choose the simple or expert coloring book at the site. Then they can choose a design, such as "flowers," click a color for each part, and click "process image" to see the results.

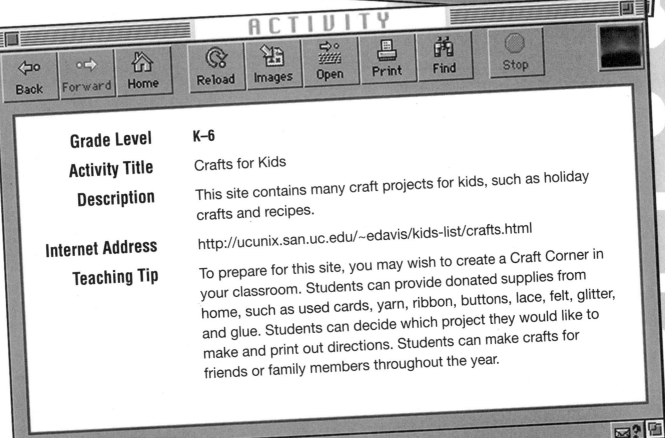

Grade Level	K–6
Activity Title	Crafts for Kids
Description	This site contains many craft projects for kids, such as holiday crafts and recipes.
Internet Address	http://ucunix.san.uc.edu/~edavis/kids-list/crafts.html
Teaching Tip	To prepare for this site, you may wish to create a Craft Corner in your classroom. Students can provide donated supplies from home, such as used cards, yarn, ribbon, buttons, lace, felt, glitter, and glue. Students can decide which project they would like to make and print out directions. Students can make crafts for friends or family members throughout the year.

Music, Art, and Dance 129

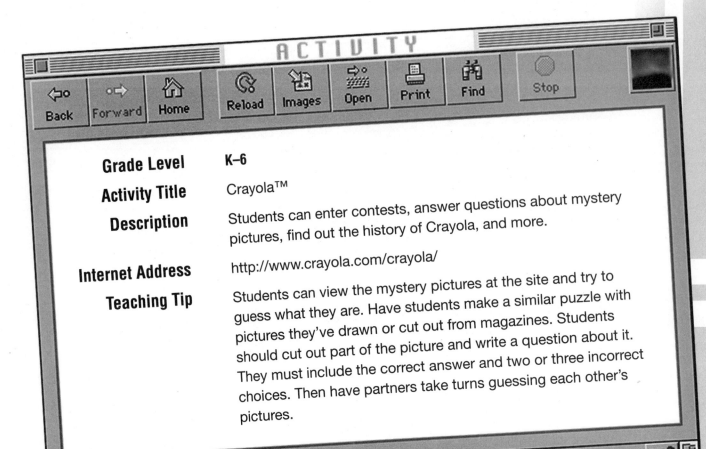

Back   Forward   Home   Reload   Images   Open   Print   Find   Stop

Grade Level	**K–6**
Activity Title	Crayola™
Description	Students can enter contests, answer questions about mystery pictures, find out the history of Crayola, and more.
Internet Address	http://www.crayola.com/crayola/
Teaching Tip	Students can view the mystery pictures at the site and try to guess what they are. Have students make a similar puzzle with pictures they've drawn or cut out from magazines. Students should cut out part of the picture and write a question about it. They must include the correct answer and two or three incorrect choices. Then have partners take turns guessing each other's pictures.

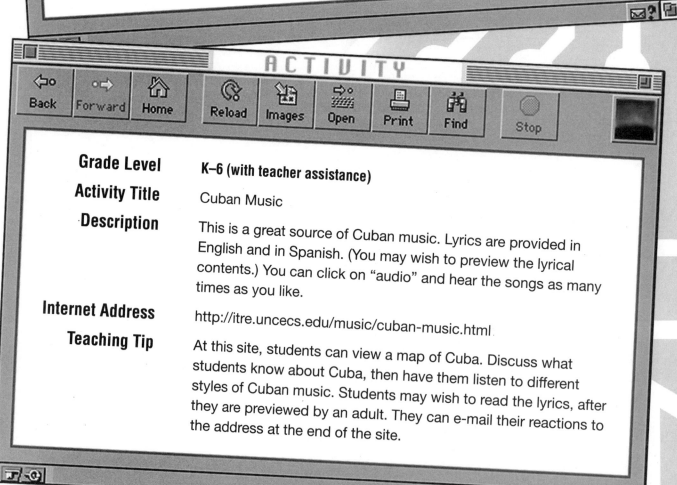

Back   Forward   Home   Reload   Images   Open   Print   Find   Stop

Grade Level	**K–6 (with teacher assistance)**
Activity Title	Cuban Music
Description	This is a great source of Cuban music. Lyrics are provided in English and in Spanish. (You may wish to preview the lyrical contents.) You can click on "audio" and hear the songs as many times as you like.
Internet Address	http://itre.uncecs.edu/music/cuban-music.html
Teaching Tip	At this site, students can view a map of Cuba. Discuss what students know about Cuba, then have them listen to different styles of Cuban music. Students may wish to read the lyrics, after they are previewed by an adult. They can e-mail their reactions to the address at the end of the site.

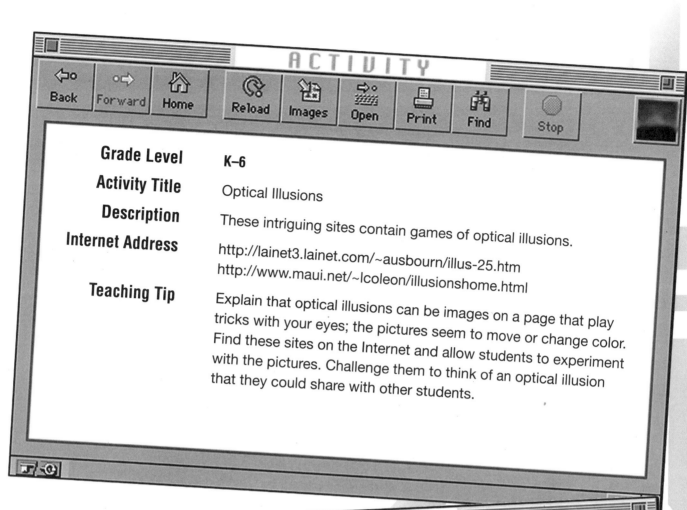

Grade Level	K–6
Activity Title	Optical Illusions
Description	These intriguing sites contain games of optical illusions.
Internet Address	http://lainet3.lainet.com/~ausbourn/illus-25.htm http://www.maui.net/~lcoleon/illusionshome.html
Teaching Tip	Explain that optical illusions can be images on a page that play tricks with your eyes; the pictures seem to move or change color. Find these sites on the Internet and allow students to experiment with the pictures. Challenge them to think of an optical illusion that they could share with other students.

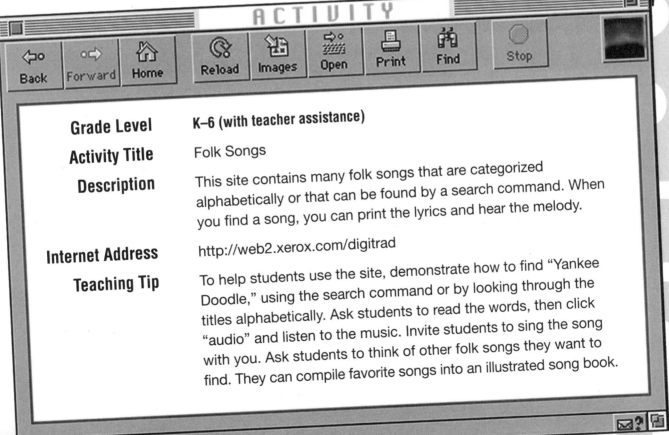

Grade Level	K–6 (with teacher assistance)
Activity Title	Folk Songs
Description	This site contains many folk songs that are categorized alphabetically or that can be found by a search command. When you find a song, you can print the lyrics and hear the melody.
Internet Address	http://web2.xerox.com/digitrad
Teaching Tip	To help students use the site, demonstrate how to find "Yankee Doodle," using the search command or by looking through the titles alphabetically. Ask students to read the words, then click "audio" and listen to the music. Invite students to sing the song with you. Ask students to think of other folk songs they want to find. They can compile favorite songs into an illustrated song book.

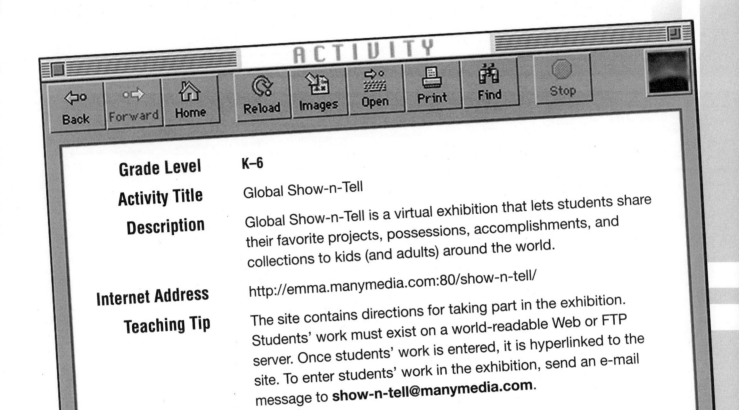

Back   Forward   Home   Reload   Images   Open   Print   Find   Stop

Grade Level   K–6

Activity Title   Global Show-n-Tell

Description   Global Show-n-Tell is a virtual exhibition that lets students share their favorite projects, possessions, accomplishments, and collections to kids (and adults) around the world.

Internet Address http://emma.manymedia.com:80/show-n-tell/

Teaching Tip   The site contains directions for taking part in the exhibition. Students' work must exist on a world-readable Web or FTP server. Once students' work is entered, it is hyperlinked to the site. To enter students' work in the exhibition, send an e-mail message to **show-n-tell@manymedia.com**.

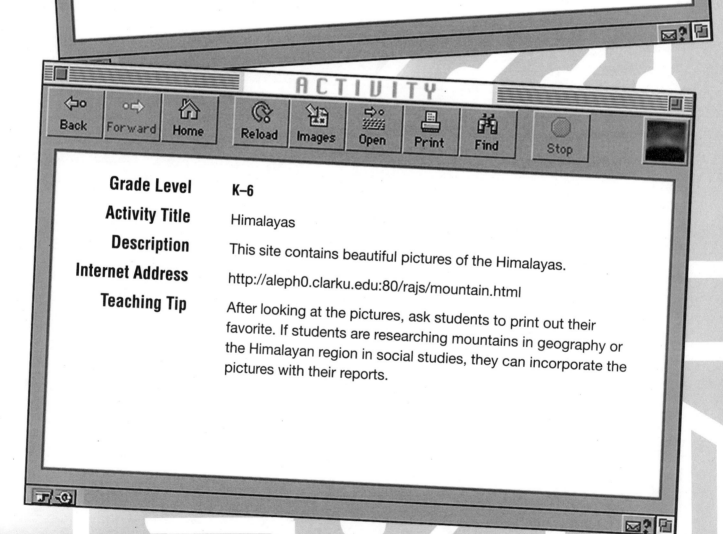

Back   Forward   Home   Reload   Images   Open   Print   Find   Stop

Grade Level   K–6

Activity Title   Himalayas

Description   This site contains beautiful pictures of the Himalayas.

Internet Address http://aleph0.clarku.edu:80/rajs/mountain.html

Teaching Tip   After looking at the pictures, ask students to print out their favorite. If students are researching mountains in geography or the Himalayan region in social studies, they can incorporate the pictures with their reports.

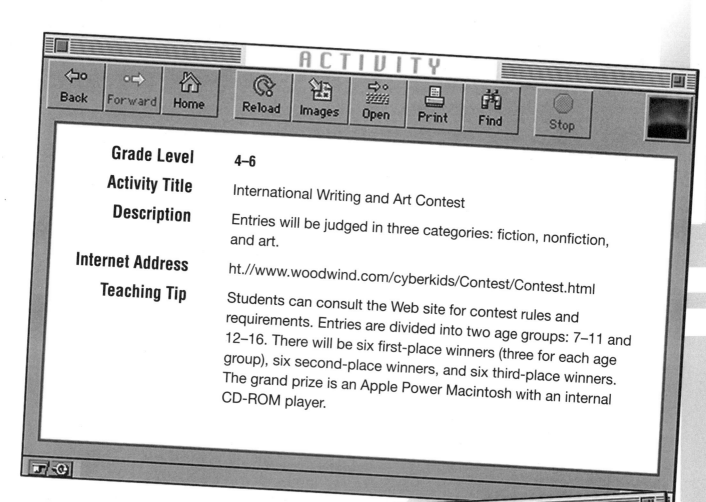

ACTIVITY

Grade Level	4–6
Activity Title	International Writing and Art Contest
Description	Entries will be judged in three categories: fiction, nonfiction, and art.
Internet Address	ht.//www.woodwind.com/cyberkids/Contest/Contest.html
Teaching Tip	Students can consult the Web site for contest rules and requirements. Entries are divided into two age groups: 7–11 and 12–16. There will be six first-place winners (three for each age group), six second-place winners, and six third-place winners. The grand prize is an Apple Power Macintosh with an internal CD-ROM player.

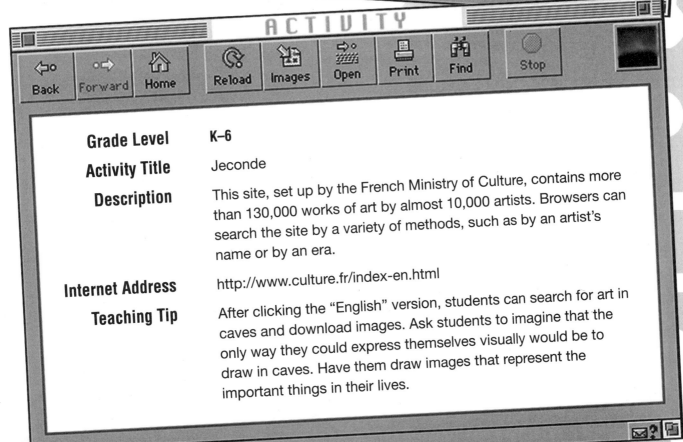

ACTIVITY

Grade Level	K–6
Activity Title	Jeconde
Description	This site, set up by the French Ministry of Culture, contains more than 130,000 works of art by almost 10,000 artists. Browsers can search the site by a variety of methods, such as by an artist's name or by an era.
Internet Address	http://www.culture.fr/index-en.html
Teaching Tip	After clicking the "English" version, students can search for art in caves and download images. Ask students to imagine that the only way they could express themselves visually would be to draw in caves. Have them draw images that represent the important things in their lives.

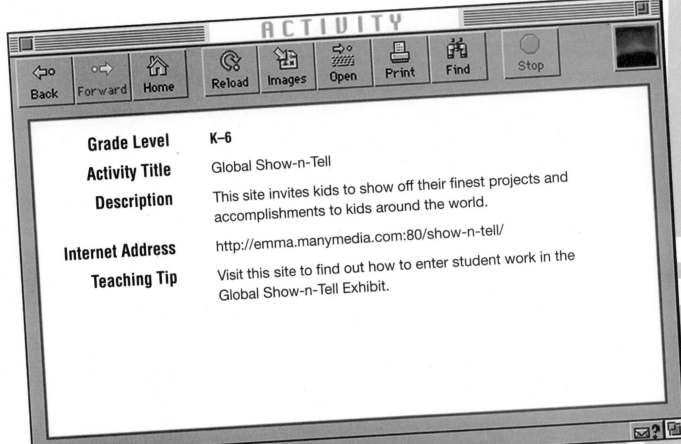

Grade Level   K–6

Activity Title   Global Show-n-Tell

Description   This site invites kids to show off their finest projects and accomplishments to kids around the world.

Internet Address   http://emma.manymedia.com:80/show-n-tell/

Teaching Tip   Visit this site to find out how to enter student work in the Global Show-n-Tell Exhibit.

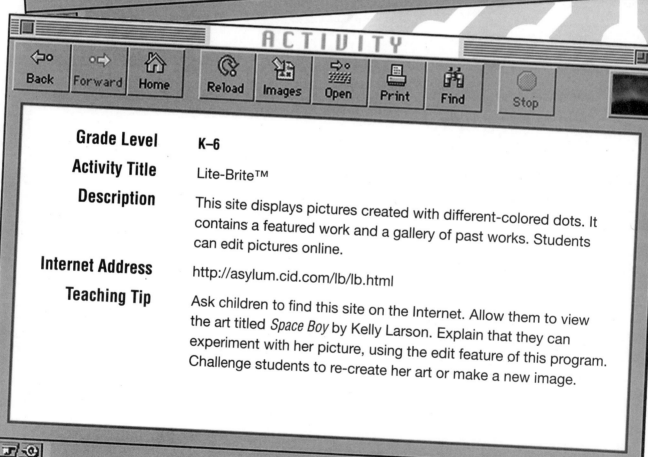

Grade Level   K–6

Activity Title   Lite-Brite™

Description   This site displays pictures created with different-colored dots. It contains a featured work and a gallery of past works. Students can edit pictures online.

Internet Address   http://asylum.cid.com/lb/lb.html

Teaching Tip   Ask children to find this site on the Internet. Allow them to view the art titled *Space Boy* by Kelly Larson. Explain that they can experiment with her picture, using the edit feature of this program. Challenge students to re-create her art or make a new image.

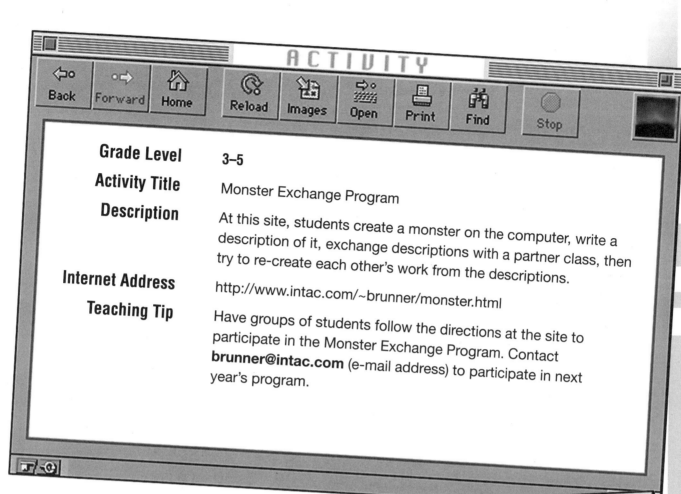

Grade Level	3–5
Activity Title	Monster Exchange Program
Description	At this site, students create a monster on the computer, write a description of it, exchange descriptions with a partner class, then try to re-create each other's work from the descriptions.
Internet Address	http://www.intac.com/~brunner/monster.html
Teaching Tip	Have groups of students follow the directions at the site to participate in the Monster Exchange Program. Contact **brunner@intac.com** (e-mail address) to participate in next year's program.

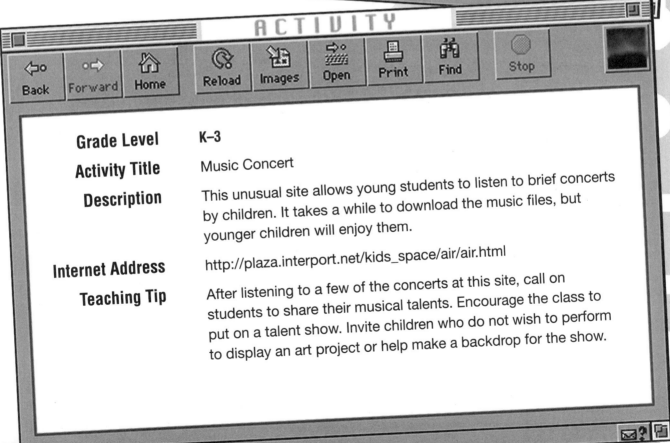

Grade Level	K–3
Activity Title	Music Concert
Description	This unusual site allows young students to listen to brief concerts by children. It takes a while to download the music files, but younger children will enjoy them.
Internet Address	http://plaza.interport.net/kids_space/air/air.html
Teaching Tip	After listening to a few of the concerts at this site, call on students to share their musical talents. Encourage the class to put on a talent show. Invite children who do not wish to perform to display an art project or help make a backdrop for the show.

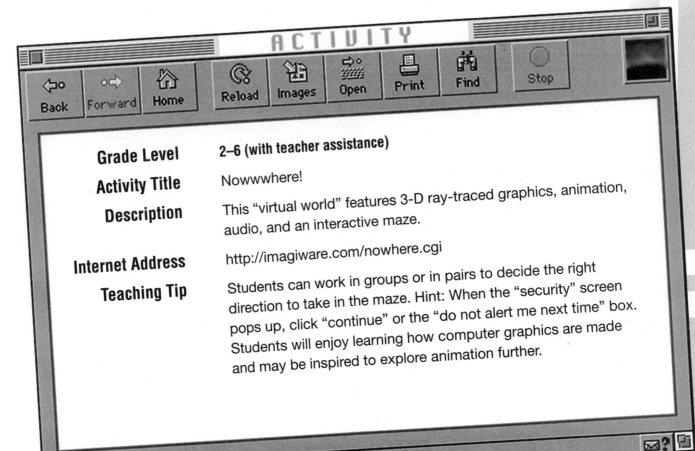

Grade Level 2–6 (with teacher assistance)

Activity Title Nowwwhere!

Description This "virtual world" features 3-D ray-traced graphics, animation, audio, and an interactive maze.

Internet Address http://imagiware.com/nowhere.cgi

Teaching Tip Students can work in groups or in pairs to decide the right direction to take in the maze. Hint: When the "security" screen pops up, click "continue" or the "do not alert me next time" box. Students will enjoy learning how computer graphics are made and may be inspired to explore animation further.

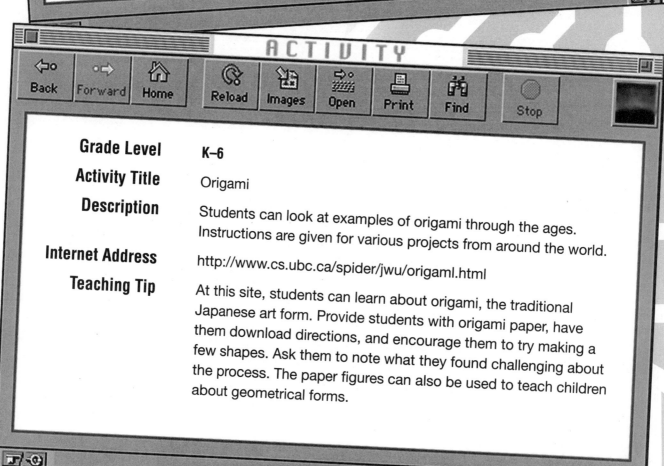

Grade Level K–6

Activity Title Origami

Description Students can look at examples of origami through the ages. Instructions are given for various projects from around the world.

Internet Address http://www.cs.ubc.ca/spider/jwu/origaml.html

Teaching Tip At this site, students can learn about origami, the traditional Japanese art form. Provide students with origami paper, have them download directions, and encourage them to try making a few shapes. Ask them to note what they found challenging about the process. The paper figures can also be used to teach children about geometrical forms.

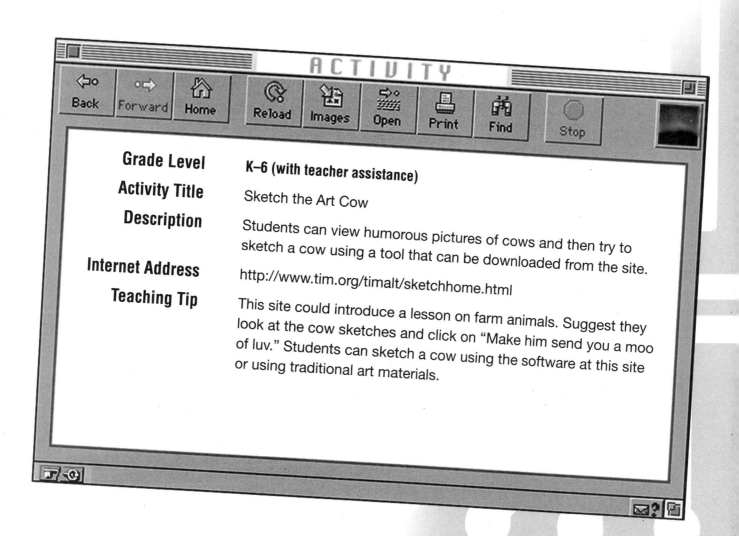

| Back | Forward | Home | Reload | Images | Open | Print | Find | Stop |

Grade Level K–6 (with teacher assistance)

Activity Title Sketch the Art Cow

Description Students can view humorous pictures of cows and then try to sketch a cow using a tool that can be downloaded from the site.

Internet Address http://www.tim.org/timalt/sketchhome.html

Teaching Tip This site could introduce a lesson on farm animals. Suggest they look at the cow sketches and click on "Make him send you a moo of luv." Students can sketch a cow using the software at this site or using traditional art materials.

Chapter 13
Projects, Organizations, and Other Resources

As introduced in Chapter 2, the Internet has tools and features that are quite useful for educators in the elementary classroom. This chapter tells how to use Internet tools to reach special projects, discussion groups, and educational materials.

Using Gopher

Gopher is a great way to browse through information on the Internet. See page 20 in Part 1 for additional information. Listed below are some of the organizations that have set up menus of items on Gopher servers.

AskERIC: Provides information for K–12 educators, such as ERIC Digests, lesson plans, archives of education-related discussions, and conference news. In response to queries, you will receive an ERIC search and full texts of any relevant ERIC Digests.
Address: Gopher: ericir.syr.edu
Telnet: ericir.syr.edu
Login: gopher

Cornucopia of Disability Information (CODI): This disability information site includes a directory of organizations and information on disability legal issues.
Address: Gopher: val-dor.cc.buffalo.edu

CTY (Center for Talented Youth): Contains newsletters, information on summer programs, writing tutorials, and other items.
Address: Gopher: jhuniverse.hcf.jhu.edu

Gopher Jewels: The University of South Carolina has compiled some of the best resources offered by Gophers, grouped by subject area. Choose these menu items at the following address: "Other Gophers and Information Resources" and "Gopher Jewels."
Address: Gopher: cwis.usc.edu

Kids Gopher (a KIDLINK service): Contains information about KIDLINK services, projects, and people. KIDLINK is a global dialog for children.
Address: Gopher: kids.duq.edu
Telnet: kids.duq.edu
Login: gopher (no password)

Project Gutenberg: Project Gutenberg is attempting to make over 10,000 public domain books freely available over the Internet as electronic text. Many sites carry the electronic texts and information. Choose these menu items at the following address: "Columbia Online Information Network," "Reference and Information Center," and "Project Gutenberg."
Address: Gopher: mizzou1.missouri.edu

Smithsonian Institution's Natural History Gopher: Offers resources and information on botany, zoology, and other subjects; the Smithsonian Biodiversity Program; and the Laboratory of Molecular Systematics.
Address: Gopher: nmnhgoph.si.edu

Groups to Join on the Internet

KIDCAFE: Youth dialog.
Subscription address: listserv@vm1.nodak.edu
Participation address: kidcafe@vm1.nodak.edu

KIDSNET: Global networking for children and educators.
Subscription address: kidsnet-request@vms.cis.pitt.edu
Participation address: kidsnet@vms.cis.pitt.edu

SIGTEL-L: A list for the Special Interest Group for Telecommunications, a service of the International Society for Technology in Education.
Subscription address: sigtel-l@unmvma.unm.edu
Participation address: sigtel-l@unmvma.unm.edu

STUMPERS-L: A forum for reference librarians, researchers, and others to pose questions that have stumped them.
Subscription address: mailserv@crf.cuis.edu
(Hint: Use the "subscribe" command just as you would with a listserv site, except enclose your e-mail address in angular brackets < and >.)
Participation address: stumpers-list@crf.cuis.edu

E-mail Lists and Discussion Groups

E-mail lists and discussion groups allow participants to debate ideas and exchange information throughout the world.

Cosndisc (Consortium for School Networking Discussion List) Subscription address: listproc@yukon.cren.org
Message address: cosndisc@yukon.cren.org

EdTech: EdTech is a discussion list for teachers, educators, students, and other individuals interested in sharing ideas and information about educational technology.
Information address: edtech@ohstvm
Bitnet subscription address: listserv@ohstvma
Internet subscription address: listerv@ohstvma.acs.ohio-state.edu

KIDSPHERE: For people interested in the development of computer networks for students and teachers.
Subscription address: kidsphere-request@vms.cis.pitt.edu
Message address: kidsphere@vms.cis.pitt.edu

TAG-L: The Talented and Gifted Education List is open to anyone interested in exchanging ideas and information related to education for the talented and the gifted.
Information address: tag-l@ndsuvm1
Bitnet subscription address: listserv@ndsuvm1
Internet subscription address: listserv@vm1.nodak.edu

Organizations and Resources

Consortium for School Networking: An organization of institutions formed to further the development and use of computer network technology in K–12 education. To join CoSN, request an application at the subscription address. To contribute ideas, lesson plans, and projects for others to access, send e-mail to the message address.

Consortium for School Networking

P.O. Box 65193

Washington, DC 20035-5193

Phone: 202-466-6296

Fax: 202-872-4318

Subscription address: info@cosn.org

Message address: ferdi@digital.cosn.org

The Educational Resources Information Center: A federally funded national information system that provides access to an extensive body of education-related literature, services, and products at all levels.

ERIC Clearinghouse on Information Resources

Center for Science and Technology

Syracuse University

Syracuse, New York 13244-4100

Phone: 315-443-9114

Fax: 315-443-5448

E-mail Address: askeric@ericir.syr.edu

NASA Spacelink: Provides access to National Science Foundation publications, phone directories, and announcements.

Telnet: spacelink.msfc.nasa.gov

Login: newuser

Password: newuser

For information on the NASA Teacher Resource Center Network, enter *g* for GO TO, then enter *TRC* or *FTP*: **spacelink.msfc.nasa.gov**.

Newton: A bulletin board system for anyone teaching or studying science, math, or computer science.

Telnet: newton.dep.anl.gov

Login: bbs

Ocean Network Information Center (OCEANIC): An interactive database of research information; includes information on the World Oceanic Circulation Experiment and schedules of research ships.

Telnet: delocn.udel.edu

Login: INFO

Teachers Applying Whole Language: Subscribers can get in touch with other teachers using the whole-language approach.

Address: listserv@listserv.arizona.edu

Collaborating with Other Educators—Web66

Web66 is a World Wide Web project for teachers and students in grades K–12. It helps educators set up Internet servers, links Web servers and educators, and helps educators find and use appropriate resources on the Web. With an international registry of K–12 schools on the Web, Web66 maintains the Internet's oldest and most comprehensive list of K–12 Web servers.

Address: http://web66.coled.umn.edu/

The pages of information on this World Wide Web server are created by students at Hillside Elementary School in Cottage Grove, Minnesota, with help from the University of Minnesota College of Education & Human Development. Hillside teachers and students incorporate the Internet into the elementary curriculum, using it to publish student work, access information, conduct research, collaborate with other schools, and share ideas.

Address: http://hillside.coled.umn.edu/